ORIENTAL STREETS

A Junior Certificate
Poetry Selection

Chosen by John White

THE EDUCATIONAL COMPANY OF IRELAND

Contents

To the teacher

The Junior Certificate English Course has as its central driving force the creation of a sensitivity to language in all its forms. The syllabus document refers to the 'innate power of words to create and suggest meaning and energise thought'. Language is intimately involved in our very notions of self and identity. Our ability to make sense of our lives, of our experiences, is bound up with the language we use. In poetry, language is at its most powerful, most sensitive, most direct. Thus poetry has a key role in the new course.

The maintenance of standards is of supreme importance. The poems in this collection have been chosen so as to be 'available' to pupils, to be within the range of their imagination and experience. A conscious attempt has been made to include poems for *girls and boys*. However, there is no devaluation of poetry by arid notions of relevance: the poems range from the complex to the transparent, from the most up-to-date to the sixteenth century, but they share that quality of 'tenderly shocking' the mind so as to expand its horizons.

How much poetry should be covered to meet the requirements of the Junior Certificate syllabus? The Intermediate Certificate course demanded twenty-five poems at Higher Level and eleven at Ordinary Level. Given that there will be a shift of focus in how poetry will be studied, the maintenance of standards demands that over the three years of the new course, at least the equivalent numbers of poems should be studied if pupils are to be adequately prepared for the Senior Cycle. Pupils should also be encouraged to learn poetry by heart.

This book deals with all of the skills and concepts demanded by the syllabus document and provides for questions and interventions which cover the domains of personal, social and cultural literacy.

The book is structured in the following way: a group of poems by a particular poet is succeeded by poems loosely dealing with a common theme. The Readings and Responses can be used for written or oral work as is appropriate. Since the new curriculum has as a major aim the integration of language and literature, the Readings and Responses include not only analysis but developmental work taking the poem as a starting-point.

It is my experience that a real boost has been given to the teaching of poetry by the New Course and we should seize this opportunity to expand and enrich our work as teachers of poetry.

John White, 1991

WORDS IN ALL THEIR GLORY!

■

The human being is *the* language animal; people control the world through words. Education, law, government, all depend on language, on the use of words. Truly words are powerful! We use words to try to understand the world, to try to understand our lives, to try to understand our feelings. The study of English involves the study of words in all their richness and variety.

Keep a list of words that interest you; these words may have an interesting sound, or an interesting meaning, or an interesting appearance.

Truth

Ladles and Jellyspoons

Words

What kind of a liar are you?

What?

Gutter Press

'Could mortal lip divine'

My life, my voice, my story

The Cheetah, my Dearest,
Is known not to cheat

■

Truth

Barrie Wade

Sticks and stones may break my bones,
but words can also hurt me.
Stones and sticks break only skin,
while words are ghosts that haunt me.

Slant and curved the word-swords fall
to pierce and stick inside me.
Bats and bricks may ache through bones,
but words can mortify me.

Pain from words has left its scar
on mind and heart that's tender.
Cuts and bruises now have healed;
it's words that I remember.

■ *Language and Concepts*

Proverb
A proberb is a short traditional saying which contains a general
truth, e.g. 'A stitch in time saves nine', 'Less said, soonest
mended'.

■ *Readings and Responses*

1   What proverb or old saying does the poet change in the first
    two lines?

2   What is meant by 'words are ghosts that haunt me'?

3   Why is it that words can hurt us so much? Is it the words
    themselves or is it what they represent?

4   What is a word? Are there other languages (sign systems)
    besides speech? Write three ways in which a message might
    be sent without speech or words.

5   'The pen is mightier than the sword'. Write a paragraph
    explaining this statement.

Ladles and Jellyspoons

Traditional English

Ladles and jellyspoons:
I come before you
To stand behind you
And tell you something
I know nothing about.

Next Thursday,
The day after Friday,
There'll be a ladies' meeting
For men only.

Wear your best clothes
If you haven't any,
And if you can come
Please stay home.

Admission is free,
You can pay at the door.
We'll give you a seat
So you can sit on the floor.

It makes no difference
Where you sit;
The kid in the gallery
Is sure to spit.

■ *Language and Concepts*

Nonsense Poem
Poetry is often about very serious subjects but there is also room
for humour and fun. A nonsense poem doesn't make sense; it is
written purely to be amusing.

■ *Readings and Responses*

1   Some pupils may know nonsense rhymes or skipping rhymes.
    Say them, write them down, or maybe tape record them.

2   Speak this poem as if it were a very important speech by a
    politician. If you didn't listen to the meanings would it appear
    to make sense?

3   When we are speaking does the accent of the speaker tell us
    anything? Are the gestures he/she makes important? How do
    clothes or hairstyles convey meaning?

Words
Alastair Reid

Words to be said on the move
FLIT
FLUCTUATE
WOBBLE
WIGGLE
SHIVER
TIPTOE
PIROUETTE
TWIRL
TEETER

Odd Words
(to be spoken out loud, for fun)
HOBNOB
BARLEY
DOG-EARED
HOPSCOTCH
WINDWARD
OAF
EGG
OBOE
NUTMEG
OBLONG

Light Words
(to be said in windy or singing moods)
ARIEL
WILLOW
SPINNAKER
WHIRR
LISSOM
SIBILANT
PETTICOAT
NIMBLE
NIB

Heavy Words
(to be used in gloom or bad weather)
DUFFLE
BLUNDERBUSS
GALOSHES
BOWL

BEFUDDLED
MUGWUM
PUMPKIN
CRUMB
BLOB

■ *Language and Concepts*

Synonym
A synonym is a word that means approximately the same as
another word: e.g. burn, blaze, flame and flare are synonyms.
Note, however, that no two words will ever mean exactly the
same. Each word has different nuances and shades of meaning:
e.g. 'blaze' suggests a lot of very bright flames, whereas 'burn'
does not necessarily involve any flames. 'Flame' could be a quiet,
gentle flame whereas 'blaze' always suggests very strong flames. A
good writer always tries to pick the exact, right word. *Roget's
Thesaurus* contains lists of words with similar meanings. Learn
how to use a Thesaurus.

■ *Readings and Responses*

1   See if you can add some other words to each group selected
    by the poet.

2   Compose poems of the same kind having the following titles:

    Wet words; Sad words; Fast words.

    Don't just pick any words. Search for interesting words.

3   'Wobble', 'wiggle' and 'twirl' are words from the first poem.
    Describe in turn what is the difference in meaning between
    these words.

4   Write down the funniest word you know.

5   Write down the longest word you know.

What kind of a liar are you?
Carl Sandburg

What kind of a liar are you?
People lie because they don't remember clear what they say.
People lie because they can't help making a story better than it was the way it happened.
People tell 'white lies' so as to be decent to others.
People lie in a pinch, hating to do it, but lying on because it might be worse.
And people lie just to be liars for a crooked personal gain.
What sort of a liar are you?
Which of these liars are you?

■ *Language and Concepts*

Leading Question
A leading question is a question which allows for only one answer. In other words, whatever answer is given the person answering the question is damning himself or herself. An example of a leading question is: 'Have you stopped criticising your friends?' If you reply 'yes' this implies that you were criticising them, but have now stopped. If you reply 'no' it means you are still criticising them.

■ *Readings and Responses*

1　'What kind of liar are you?' is a leading question. Explain why it is.

2　Would you say there is some kind of truth in the statement that we are all liars? Explain what you mean.

3　Make distinctions between the various kinds of lies mentioned in this poem. Which are really evil and which not evil at all?

4　If we were always to say exactly what was in our minds would this cause problems for us — at school, with our friends, at home? Give examples.

5　Do advertisements tell the truth? Prepare a talk dealing with this question.

What?

Ivor Cutler

Where
man has not been
to give
them names
objects
on desert islands
do not
know what they are.
Taking no chances
they stand still
and wait
quietly excited
for hundreds
of
thousands of
years.

■ *Language and Concepts*

Neologism
A neologism is a new word introduced into the language. In the
last twenty years, for example, the following words have entered
the English language: silicon chip, supergrass, yuppie, video, fax.
Language must constantly change because the world constantly
changes.

■ *Readings and Responses*

1   What does this poem say to us about the relationship between
    words and things? Which comes first — the object or the
    name of the object?

2   Did you ever try to make up a private language of your own?
    Try to do this for the objects in the classroom and then try to
    compose a sentence in this new language. What are the
    problems?

3   Make a list of as many neologisms as you can.

4   Do animals have a language? If so, how does it differ from
    human language?

5   Language is vitally important for everybody but are there
    particular occupations in which language is particularly
    important?

Gutter Press

Paul Dehn

News Editor: Peer Confesses,
Bishop Undresses,
Torso Wrapped in Rug,
Girl Guide Throttled,
Baronet Bottled,
J.P. Goes to Jug.

But yesterday's story's
Old and hoary.
Never mind who got hurt.
No use grieving,
Let's get weaving.
What's the latest dirt?

Diplomat Spotted,
Scout Garrotted,
Thigh Discovered in Bog,
Wrecks Off Barmouth,
Sex in Yarmouth,
Woman in Love with Dog,
Eminent Hostess shoots her Guests,
Harrogate Lovebird Builds Two Nests.

Cameraman: *Builds two nests?*
Shall I get a picture of the lovebird singing?
Shall I get a picture of her pretty little eggs?
Shall I get a picture of her babies?

News Editor: No!
Go and get a picture of her legs.

Beast Slays Beauty
Priest Flays Cutie,
Cupboard Shows Tell-Tale Stain,
Mate Drugs Purser,
Dean Hugs Bursar,
Mayor Binds Wife with Chain,
Elderly Monkey Marries for Money,
Jilted Junky Says 'I want My Honey'.

Cameraman: *'Want my honey?'*
Shall I get a picture of the pollen flying?
Shall I get a picture of the golden dust?
Shall I get a picture of a queen bee?

News Editor: No!
                            Go and get a picture of her bust.

                            Judge Gets Frisky,
                            Nun Drinks Whisky,
                            Baby Found Burnt in Cot,
                            Show Girl Beaten,
                            Duke Leaves Eton —

Cameraman: *Newspaper Man Gets Shot!*
                            May all things clean
                            And fresh and green
                            Have mercy upon your soul,
                            Consider yourself paid
                            by the hole my bullet made —

News Editor
(dying):   Come and get a picture of the hole.

■ *Language and Concepts*

Sensationalism
Sensationalism is the crude presentation and exploitation of violence, horror and sex in order to sell newspapers. In a sensationalist story everything is made to appear exciting, even if it is not. The most famous sensationalist headline in recent times was 'Gotcha' in *The Sun* to describe the death of over 300 sailors during The Falklands War.

■ *Readings and Responses*

1 'Never mind who got hurt'. What does this tell us about the News Editor?

2 'What's the latest dirt?' Does good news sell newspapers?

3 Sensationalism exploits the bizarre, the unusual, the extreme in headlines. The following headline was voted the most boring ever: 'Small earthquake in Chile. Nobody killed.'

   Why is this headline not sensationalist?

4 Is the News Editer totally obsessed with his work? Look at the last lines of the poem.

5 Write some sensationalist headlines to suit some current news stories.

'Could mortal lip divine'

Emily Dickinson

Could mortal lip divine
The undeveloped Freight
Of a delivered syllable
'Twould crumble with the weight.

■ *Language and Concepts*

Style in writing
The best definition of style is 'proper words in proper places'.
When writing we must always search out the word which
describes most clearly what we mean. We must never be slapdash
or careless in the words we choose.

■ *Readings and Responses*

1   In this poem the poet says that every syllable we utter may
    contain important meanings which we don't fully realise. Can
    you think of words a person might say which would change
    their lives? Think for example, of the words said in the
    marriage ceremony.

2   Does the way a person speaks tell us anything about their
    personality? Think of accent, vocabulary, speed, noise level.
    Give examples from people you know or from people in the
    media.

3   'I wish I hadn't said that.' Write a paragraph suggested by
    these words.

4   'I only wish I had said it.' Write a paragraph suggested by
    these words.

5   'A good listener is a good friend.' Do you agree?

My life, my voice, my story

Davoren Hanna

Davoren Hanna was thought, for many years, to be mentally retarded because, accompanying his major physical disabilities, he was unable to speak. Language was the key which released him from the prison of isolation. He has said: 'My first word was my greatest achievement, my Everest,' and 'Words define my world as feet define the dancer's.'

> The moon blackened at my birth
> and long night's cry began.
> Pain became my bed-fellow
> and despair my song.
> God disappeared behind the clouds;
> I lost my star-signpost to hope.
>
> Light found a chink to peep through
> when poems were read to my starved soul.
> Loneliness brought moments of repose;
> lines poured through my veins
> and love glimmered on my tongue.
> Little birds became my inspiration.
>
> Left with my own silent melody,
> I painted notes of long-forgotten tunes
> trembling in my trapped heart.
> Light burst through my dark mouth
> and myriad songs flew heavenwards.
> I was poised for flight...

■ *Readings and Responses*

1   What is meant by the lines 'The moon blackened at my birth and long night's cry began'?

2   What gave hope to his 'starved soul'?

3   How was his melody 'silent'?

4   'I was poised for flight ...' What is meant by this? Why is the sentence left unfinished?

5   Explain what is meant by the title.

The Cheetah, My Dearest,
Is known not to cheat

George Barker

The cheetah, my dearest, is known not to cheat:
the Tiger possesses no tie;
The horse-fly, of course, was never a horse;
the lion will not tell a lie.

The turkey, though perky, was never a Turk;
nor the monkey ever a monk;
the mandrel, though like one, was never a man,
but some men are like him, when drunk.

The springbok, dear thing, was not born in the Spring;
The walrus will not build a wall.
No badger is bad; no adder can add.
There is no truth in these things at all.

■ *Language and Concepts*

'Play' on words
Sometimes a writer plays with words, with their sound and meaning so as to create a humorous effect. We often do this ourselves in jokes and riddles.

■ *Readings and Responses*

1   This poem is meant to be humorous but it is also gently suggesting that words can deceive. Pick out three examples given in the poem of words that could confuse a young child or person learning English.

2   Language is full of deceptions. Can you think of words which have the same sound but different meanings — e.g. palm (of your hand) and palm (tree), soul (divine soul) and sole (of your foot)?

3   The game 'Chinese Whispers' illustrates how a message can be confused in the telling. In this game a message is passed from one person to another and to another and so on. By the time the message has reached the last person what do you think may have happened?

4   Take, for example, the word 'cat'. How can this one word cover all the different varieties of cats — the different breeds, shapes and colours?

SEAMUS HEANEY

Seamus Heaney was born in 1939 in County Derry. He has worked as a teacher and University lecturer. He lives in Dublin but spends part of every year teaching at Harvard University in the U.S.A. He was recently elected Professor of Poetry at Oxford University. He is married to Marie Devlin and they have three children. Seamus Heaney is regarded as one of the finest writers currently writing in the English language.

Personal Helicon

Digging

The Diviner

Blackberry-Picking

Bye-Child

When all the Others

The Cool that Came off Sheets

Mid-Term Break

Personal Helicon

For Michael Longley

Seamus Heaney

As a child, they could not keep me from wells
And old pumps with buckets and windlasses.
I loved the dark drop, the trapped sky, the smells
Of waterweed, fungus and dank moss.

One, in a brickyard, with a rotted board top.
I savoured the rich crash when a bucket
Plummeted down at the end of a rope.
So deep you saw no reflection in it.

A shallow one under a dry stone ditch
Fructified like any aquarium.
When you dragged out long roots from the soft mulch
A white face hovered over the bottom.

Others had echoes, gave back your own call
With a clean new music in it. And one
Was scaresome for there, out of ferns and tall
Foxgloves, a rat slapped across my reflection.

Now, to pry into roots, to finger slime,
To stare, big-eyed Narcissus, into some spring
Is beneath all adult dignity. I rhyme
To see myself, to set the darkness echoing.

■ *Readings and Responses*

1   Mount Helicon in Greece was the home of the Goddesses of poetry. The Goddesses inspired poets. The title 'Personal Helicon' means personal inspiration. What fascinated and inspired the poet as a child?

2   Pick out the lines which appeal to each of the senses in turn.

3   What fascinates the poet now that he is an adult?

4   In what way is the adult poet similar to the child?

5   What is meant by the phrase 'to set the darkness echoing'?

6   Write a paragraph (or more) about an object or place that fascinates and intrigues you in the way that 'wells' intrigued Heaney.

Digging

Seamus Heaney

Between my finger and my thumb
The squat pen rests; snug as a gun.

Under my window, a clean rasping sound
When the spade sinks into gravelly ground:
My father, digging. I look down

Till his straining rump among the flowerbeds
Bends low, comes up twenty years away
Stooping in rhythm through potato drills
Where he was digging.

The coarse boot nestled on the lug, the shaft
Against the inside knee was levered firmly.
He rooted out tall tops, buried the bright edge deep
To scatter new potatoes that we picked
Loving their cool hardness in our hands.

By God, the old man could handle a spade.
Just like his old man.

My grandfather cut more turf in a day
Than any other man on Toner's bog.
Once I carried him milk in a bottle
Corked sloppily with paper. He straightened up
To drink it, then fell to right away
Nicking and slicing neatly, heaving sods
Over his shoulder, going down and down
For the good turf. Digging.

The cold smell of potato mould, the squelch and slap
Of soggy peat, the curt cuts of an edge
Through living roots awaken in my head.
But I've no spade to follow men like them.

Between my finger and my thumb
The squat pen rests.
I'll dig with it.

■ *Language and Concepts*

Metaphor
A metaphor is a comparison without using the words 'like' or 'as'.
A word is transferred from its context to another context, e.g. 'The
boat ploughed through the waves.' A boat does not literally

'plough' in the sense of ploughing a field so 'the boat ploughed through the waves' is a metaphor. In this poem the poet says he is going to 'dig' with his pen. This is metaphorical use of language.

■ *Readings and Responses*

1   What work does the poet remember his father doing?

2   What work does he remember his grandfather doing?

3   How is the poet going to dig with his pen? Where will he dig?

4   Pick out the words or phrases that appeal to the various senses.

5   Describe in detail a job you have done which you enjoyed doing.

The Diviner

Seamus Heaney

Cut from the green hedge a forked hazel stick
That he held tight by the arms of the V:
Circling the terrain, hunting the pluck
Of water, nervous, but professionally

Unfussed. The pluck came sharp as a sting.
The rod jerked down with precise convulsions,
Spring water suddenly broadcasting
Through a green aerial its secret stations.

The bystanders would ask to have a try.
He handed them the rod without a word.
It lay dead in their grasp till nonchalantly
He gripped expectant wrists. The hazel stirred.

■ *Language and Concepts*

Simile

A simile is a comparison using the words 'like' or 'as', e.g. 'The branches of the tree were like twisted hands.' 'His fingers were as slim as a pianist's.' Write out ten interesting similes. Try to avoid clichés such as 'as black as coal'.

1   There is one very unusual word in the first verse. What is this unusual word? Say what you think it means.

2   Pick out the simile in the second verse. What does it tell us?

3   What is meant by 'broadcasting/Through a green aerial its secret stations'?

4   What is the effect of the short last sentence?

5   The diviner has an unusual job. Give an account of an unusual job or skill that you know about.

Blackberry-Picking

For Philip Hobsbaum

Seamus Heaney

Late August, given heavy rain and sun
For a full week, the blackberries would ripen.
At first, just one, a glossy purple clot
Among others, red, green, hard as a knot.
You ate that first one and its flesh was sweet
Like thickened wine: summer's blood was in it
Leaving stains upon the tongue and lust for
Picking. Then red ones inked up and that hunger
Sent us out with milk-cans, pea-tins, jam-pots
Where briars scratched and wet grass bleached our boots.
Round hayfields, cornfields and potato-drills
We trekked and picked until the cans were full,
Until the tinkling bottom had been covered
With green ones, and on top big dark blobs burned
Like a plate of eyes. Our hands were peppered
With thorn pricks, our palms sticky as Bluebeard's.

We hoarded the fresh berries in the byre.
But when the bath was filled we found a fur,
A rat-grey fungus, glutting on our cache.
The juice was stinking too. Once off the bush
The fruit fermented, the sweet flesh would turn sour.
I always felt like crying. It wasn't fair
That all the lovely canfuls smelt of rot.
Each year I hoped they'd keep, knew they would not.

The Five Senses
We learn about the world through our five senses. The five senses
are sight, touch, taste, sound, smell. Try to imagine what the
world would be like without one of each of the senses in turn.
Poets try to tell us what the world is like so they must appeal to
our senses. The five senses can also be called the visual sense,
the tactile, the gustatory, the aural and the olfactory. In your
writing try to appeal to the senses of the reader.

■ *Readings and Responses*

1   The poet appeals to the five senses. Pick out the lines in
    which each sense is evoked.

2   Pick out all the colour words.

3   Write out ten colours as powerful as 'rat-grey'.

4   What lesson did the blackberry-picker learn?

5   Is this poem optimistic or pessimistic?

Bye-Child

*He was discovered in the henhouse where she had confined him.
He was incapable of saying anything.*

Seamus Heaney

When the lamp glowed,
A yolk of light
In their back window,
The child in the outhouse
Put his eye to a chink —

Little henhouse boy,
Sharp-faced as new moons
Remembered, your photo still

Glimpsed like a rodent
On the floor of my mind,

Little moon man,
Kennelled and faithful
At the foot of the yard,
Your frail shape, luminous,
Weightless, is stirring the dust,

The cobwebs, old droppings
Under the roosts
And dry smells from scraps
She put through your trapdoor
Morning and evening.

After those footsteps, silence;
Vigils, solitudes, fasts,
Unchristened tears,
A puzzled love of the light.
But now you speak at last

With a remote mime
Of something beyond patience,
Your gaping wordless proof
Of lunar distances
Travelled beyond love.

■ *Language and Concepts*

Image
An image is a picture or suggestion put into your mind by the
words of the poet. 'A yolk of light' puts into our mind the picture
or image of the orange/yellow light seen glowing in the back
window; 'like a rodent' puts into our mind the image or picture of
a 'rat-like' boy. The words of a good writer should create images
in our minds.

■ *Readings and Responses*

1   Why is the word 'yolk' more expressive than other words the
    poet might have used? Think of where the boy is confined.

2   Now that the child is released will he be able to tell of his
    experiences?

3   If the child had language what differences would there be?

4   Is this an horrific poem?

5   In what sense is the bye-child different to an animal?

When all the Others

Seamus Heaney

When all the others were away at Mass
I was all hers as we peeled potatoes.
They broke the silence, let fall one by one
Like solder weeping off the soldering iron;
Cold comforts set between us, things to share
Gleaming in a bucket of clean water.
And again let fall. Little pleasant splashes
From each other's work would bring us to our senses.

So while the parish priest at her bedside
Went hammer and tongs at the prayers for the dying
And some were responding and some crying
I remembered her head bent towards my head,
Her breath in mine, our fluent dipping knives —
Never closer the whole rest of our lives.

■ *Language and Concepts*

Sonnet
A Petrarchan or Italian sonnet is a poem of fourteen lines. It is divided into two parts: the first eight lines are called the octave and the last six lines are called the sestet. In the octave one aspect of the subject is treated and in the sestet there is a new angle or development.

■ *Readings and Responses*

1   Have you ever worked with somebody or played a game with somebody in such a way that you felt in harmony with them as the poet and his mother felt in harmony with one another?

2   Pick out your favourite time of the week — a period of not more than two hours. Describe it.

3   Why did the poet and his mother not speak as they were peeling the potatoes?

4   Is there love in this poem?

5   How many of the senses are appealed to in this poem? Go through each of the senses and try to find examples.

The Cool that Came off Sheets

Seamus Heaney

The cool that came off sheets just off the line
Made me think the damp must still be in them
But when I took my corners of the linen
And pulled against her, first straight down the hem
And then diagonally, then flapped and shook
The fabric like a sail in a cross-wind,
They made a dried-out undulating thwack.
So we'd stretch and fold and end up hand to hand
For a split second as if nothing had happened
For nothing had that had not always happened
Beforehand, day by day, just touch and go,
Coming close again by holding back
In moves where I was x and she was o
Inscribed in sheets she'd sewn from ripped-out flour sacks.

■ *Language and Concepts*

Onomatopoeia
Language is a system of signs and words which usually bear no
relation to what they refer to. As Shakespeare said 'A rose by any
other name is just as sweet'. There are, however, some words
which are similar to the sound they are describing, e.g. 'buzz' is
like the sound of the flying bee and the word 'cuckoo' echoes the
sound made by the cuckoo. When a word makes the sound it
describes this is called onomatopoeia.

■ *Readings and Responses*

1   In pairs mime the folding of the sheets.

2   Pick out the onomatopoeic word in the poem. Why is it such a
good word?

3   Do the mother and the poet speak to each other as they are
folding the sheets?

4   What does the poet mean by the line 'Coming close again by
holding back'?

5   This is a poem about a moment of wordless, intimate
communication. Do you agree?

Mid-Term Break

Seamus Heaney

I sat all morning in the college sick bay
Counting bells knelling classes to a close.
At two o'clock our neighbours drove me home.

In the porch I met my father crying —
He had always taken funerals in his stride —
And Big Jim Evans saying it was a hard blow.

The baby cooed and laughed and rocked the pram
When I came in, and I was embarrassed
By old men standing up to shake my hand

And tell me they were 'sorry for my trouble'.
Whispers informed strangers I was the eldest,
Away at school, as my mother held my hand

In hers and coughed out angry tearless sighs.
At ten o'clock the ambulance arrived
With the corpse, stanched and bandaged by the nurses.

Next morning I went up into the room. Snowdrops
And candles soothed the bedside; I saw him
For the first time in six weeks. Paler now,

Wearing a poppy bruise on his left temple,
He lay in the four foot box as in his cot.
No gaudy scars, the bumper knocked him clear.
A four foot box, a foot for every year.

■ *Readings and Responses*

1 This is a poem of great poignancy. What are the most touching, almost heartbreaking, details?

2 How does the whole community try to share the sorrow of the family?

RHYTHM

Rhythm
The rhythm of a poem is linked to the sound. Rhythm is the regular occurrence of a particular beat or pattern of stressed and unstressed syllables. The rhythm should be in harmony with the meaning: thus a joyous poem might have a lilting rhythm, while a sad poem might have a slow, mournful rhythm.

Night Mail

From a Railway Carriage

Night Mail

W.H. Auden

This is the night mail crossing the border,
Bringing the cheque and the postal order,
Letters for the rich, letters for the poor,
The shop at the corner and the girl next door.
Pulling up Beattock, a steady climb —
The gradient's against her, but she's on time.

Past cotton grass and moorland boulder,
Shovelling white steam over her shoulder,
Snorting noisily as she passes
Silent miles of wind-bent grasses.
Birds turn their heads as she approaches,
Stare from the bushes at her blank-faced coaches.
Sheepdogs cannot turn her course,
They slumber on with paws across.
In the farm she passes no one wakes,
But a jug in the bedroom gently shakes.

Dawn freshens, the climb is done.
Down towards Glasgow she descends
Towards the steam tugs yelping down the glade of cranes,
Towards the fields of apparatus, the furnaces
Set on the dark plain like gigantic chessmen,
All Scotland waits for her:
In the dark glen, beside the pale-green lochs,
Men long for news.

Letters of thanks, letters from banks,
Letters of joy from girl and boy,
Receipted bills, and invitations
To inspect new stock or visit relations,
And applications for situations
And timid lovers' declarations
And gossip, gossip from all the nations,
News circumstantial, news financial,
Letters with holiday snaps to enlarge in,

Letters with faces scrawled in the margin,
Letters from uncles, cousins and aunts,
Letters to Scotland from the South of France,
Letters of condolence to Highlands and Lowlands,
Written on paper of every hue,
The pink, the violet, the white and the blue,
The chatty, the catty, the boring, adoring,

The cold and official and the heart's outpouring.
Clever, stupid, short and long,
The typed and the printed and the spelt all wrong.

Thousands are still asleep
Dreaming of terrifying monsters,
Or a friendly tea beside the band at Cranston's or Crawford's:
Asleep in working Glasgow, asleep in well-set Edinburgh,
Asleep in granite Aberdeen,
They continue their dreams;
But shall wake soon and long for letters,
And none will hear the postman's knock
Without a quickening of the heart,
For who can hear and feel himself forgotten?

■ *Readings and Responses*

1   What does the sound or rhythm of this poem try to imitate?

2   Is there a change of rhythm in the third verse? How would
    you describe the rhythm of this verse?

3   There are some very good visual images in the second verse.
    Pick the two which are most vivid and describe them.

4   There is an appeal to the sense of hearing in the second verse.
    Describe it.

5   What do the last three lines of the poem tell us about human
    beings? Is it a pity that people write fewer letters to each other
    nowadays?

From a Railway Carriage

Robert Louis Stevenson

Faster than fairies, faster than witches,
Bridges and houses, hedges and ditches;
And charging along like troops in a battle,
All through the meadows the horses and cattle;
All of the sights of the hill and the plain
Fly as thick as driving rain;
And ever again, in the wink of an eye,
Painted stations whistle by.

Here is a child who clambers and scrambles,
All by himself and gathering brambles;
Here is a tramp who stands and gazes;
And there is the green for stringing the daisies!
Here is a cart run away in the road
Lumping along with man and load;
And here is a mill, and there is a river:
Each a glimpse and gone for ever !

■ *Readings and Responses*

1   What does the sound or rhythm of this poem try to imitate?

2   What is the simile in lines three and four?

3   Pick out the two most vivid scenes that can be seen from the railway carriage.

4   Which of the two poems *Night Mail* or *From a Railway Carriage* creates the sense of a railway journey the better? Give reasons for your answer.

5   Which kind of travel do you enjoy most — bus, rail, car, plane, ship. Why? Write or tell about a journey you went on.

SCHOOLDAYS — ARE THEY THE HAPPIEST DAYS?

■

A school pupil once said that if schooldays are the happiest days of our lives, then the rest of life must be pretty awful. As with all generalisations, the statement 'schooldays are the happiest days of your life' contains an element of truth. For good or ill, school is very important and the poems which follow deal with both the negative and positive aspects of school life.

Wee Hughie

Geographic Landmarks

First Day at School

My Parents kept me from Children who were Rough

Back in the Playground Blues

Fight

Truant

The Best of School

The Village Schoolmaster

■

Wee Hughie

Elizabeth Shane

He's gone to school, Wee Hughie,
    An' him not four,
Sure I saw the fright was in him
    When he left the door.

But he took a hand of Denny
    An' a hand of Dan,
Wi' Joe's owld coat upon him —
    Och, the poor wee man!

He cut the quarest figure,
    More stout nor thin,
An' trottin' right an' steady,
    Wi' his toes turned in.

I watched him to the corner
    O' the big turf stack,
An' the more his feet went forrit,
    Still his head turned back.

He was lookin', would I call him,
    Och, me heart was woe —
Sure it's lost I am without him,
    But he be to go.

I followed to the turnin'
    When he passed it by,
God help him, he was cryin'
    And maybe so was I.

■ *Language and Concepts*

Dialect
English is spoken in many different countries, in many different parts of the world. In all these countries there are different accents, pronunciations and different words. These different varieties of the language are called dialects.

■ *Readings and Responses*

1   Describe Wee Hughie on his way to school for the first time.

2   How does Hughie's mother feel now that he is going to school?

3   Pick out two dialect words used in this poem.

4   Make a list of words that are used only in Ireland (this version of English, particular to Ireland, is called Hiberno-English), e.g. the crack (meaning sport and fun), cat (meaning rough), culchie (country person), etc.

5   Do you remember your first day at school? Write about it, describing your feelings.

Geographic Landmarks

Davoren Hanna

The best of all subjects is geography!
Fearsome distances disappear into coloured
shapes like felt-animal jigsaws.
Rivers wriggle like inky worms
across the sellotaped pages of my atlas.
Lakes and mountains nudge each other
sideways as they fight for space
upon my topsy-turvy sandwiched map.
Would Gulliver step on little towns
if the world was as small as this?
Quiet spaces surround me as I ponder,
wide prairies await me when I wander.

■ *Readings and Responses*

1   Why is geography the poet's favourite subject? Look particularly at the last two lines. Read the note about Davoren Hanna on page 11.

2   Do you think the two similes are vivid?

3   Read the other poem in this book by Davoren Hanna on page 11.

4   Explain precisely what an atlas is.

5   Write your own version: The best of all subjects ...

First Day at School

Roger McGough

A millionbillionwillion miles from home
Waiting for the bell to go. (To go where?)
Why are they all so big, other children?
So noisy? So much at home they
must have been born in uniform.
Lived all their lives in playgrounds.
Spent the years inventing games
that don't let me in. Games
that are rough, that swallow you up.

And the railings.
All around, the railings:
Are they to keep out the wolves and monsters?
Things that carry off and eat children?
Things you don't take sweets from?
Perhaps they're to stop us getting out.
Running away from the lessins. Lessin.
What does a lessin look like?
Sounds small and slimy.
They keep them in glassrooms.
Whole rooms made out of glass. Imagine.

I wish I could remember my name.
Mummy said it would come in useful.
Like wellies. When there's puddles.
Yellowwellies. I wish she was here.
I think my name is sewn on somewhere.
Perhaps the teacher will read it for me.
Tea-cher. The one who makes the tea.

■ *Readings and Responses*

1 How would you describe the feelings of this child on his/her first day at school?

2 'Fear of the unknown' is terrifying. Look at the second verse and in particular the words 'railings' and 'lessins'. Why is the child terrified of them?

3 Terror and humour seem to be opposites but sometimes they exist together. Is this so in this poem? Where does this occur?

4 The child doesn't know what a 'lessin' is. Are there any words that you have heard which confuse and fascinate you but you

still don't know the meaning of them? Write down some of
them.

5   Were there differences between your first day at primary
    school and your first day at post-primary school? Prepare a
    talk or write about them, comparing and contrasting the two
    days.

My Parents kept me from Children who were Rough

Stephen Spender

My parents kept me from children who were rough
Who threw words like stones and who wore torn clothes.
Their thighs showed through rags. They ran in the street
And climbed cliffs and stripped by the country streams.

I feared more than tigers their muscles like iron
Their jerking hands and their knees tight on my arms.
I feared the salt coarse pointing of those boys
Who copied my lisp behind me on the road.

They were lithe, they sprang out behind hedges
Like dogs to bark at my world. They threw mud
While I looked the other way, pretending to smile.
I longed to forgive them, but they never smiled.

■ *Readings and Responses*

1   Two contrasting lifestyles are presented in this poem. What
    are they?

2   Discuss the view that this is a poem about isolation and
    loneliness.

3   What do you think of the attitude of the parents of the boy?

4   Why did the 'rough' children feel antagonistic towards the
    boy? Were they justified?

5   The social class a person comes from is not important in
    Ireland today. Discuss.

Back in the Playground Blues

Adrian Mitchell

Dreamed I was in a school playground I was about
      four feet high
Yes dreamed I was back in the playground and
      standing about four feet high
The playground was three miles long and the playground
      was five miles wide.
It was broken black tarmac with a high wire fence all
      around
Broken black dusty tarmac with a high fence running
      all around
And it had a special name to it, they called it
      The Killing Ground

Got a mother and a father they're a thousand miles away
The Rulers of the Killing Ground are coming out to play
Everyone thinking: who they going to play with today

You get it for being Jewish
Get it for being black
Get it for being chicken
Get it for fighting back
You get it for being big and fat
Get it for being small
Oh those who get it get it and get it
For any damn thing at all

Sometimes they take a beetle tear off its six legs one by one
Beetle on its black back rocking in the lunchtime sun
But a beetle can't beg for mercy, a beetle's not half the fun
Heard a deep voice talking, it had that iceberg sound
'It prepares them for a life' — but I have never found
Any place in my life that's worse than The Killing Ground

■ *Language and Concepts*

'The Blues'
'The Blues' is a type of music originally composed and sung by
black people in the Southern States of the United States of
America. Because the lives of black people had been harsh and
cruel 'the Blues' tend to be about the sad and tragic aspects of
life. Modern rock-and-roll is loosely derived from the rhythms of
this music.

1 Prepare a class reading of this poem. The section beginning 'You get it for being Jewish' could be read by seven different people, each with a separate line.

2 'Schooldays are the happiest days of your life.' Does the speaker in this poem think so?

3 'It prepares them for life.' Why has this statement 'an iceberg sound'?

4 My Worst Day in School. Write a description of it.

5 Bullying in school. Is it a serious problem?

Fight

Barrie Wade

'A scrap! A scrap!'
The tingle in the scalp
starts us running.

The shout drains
our playground just as though
a plug was pulled

here in the space
in which two twisted, furious
bodies writhe.

Rules will not prise
these savages apart.
No ref will interpose

with shouts of 'Break!'
This contest has one single
vicious round

of grab and grapple,
wrestle, thump and scrabble,
flail and scratch.

We take no sides.
Our yells are wolves howling
for blood of any kind.

Our fingers clench.
The thrill claws in our throats
like raging thirst.

The whistle shrills
and splits our pack. The circle
heaves and shatters.

The fighters still
are blind and deaf, won't hear
or see until,

parted, they go limp
as cubs drawn by the scruff
from some hot lair.

Now they are tame,
Standing outside Sir's room
grinning their shame.

Chastened, we feel
the snarls of wildness
stifle in us.

■ *Language and Concepts*

Slang
Slang is colloquial, sometimes coarse language which is not used in polite conversation or in formal situations. Slang can be rich and powerful but must only be used in the right context. In your writing, you can use slang if you are quoting what somebody said or if you are happy that it is suitable in the context. The word 'scrap' in the poem *Fight* is a mild slang word.

■ *Readings and Responses*

1   Explain the simile in verse two.

2   Which verse has action words describing the fight? Pick out the two best action words. Say why you picked them out.

3   Pick out four words which are usually used with regard to animals. Why is animal imagery used in this poem?

4   What are your views on boxing as a sport? Prepare a talk giving your views.

5   Have you ever seen a fight like the one described in the poem? Try to describe it so that the reader will be able to see it in his or her mind's eye.

Truant

Phoebe Hesketh

Sing a song of sunlight
My pocket's full of sky —
Starling's egg for April
Jay's feather for July.
And here's a thorn bush three bags full
Of drift-white wool.

They call him dunce, and yet he can discern
Each mouse-brown bird,
And call its name and whistle back its call.
And spy among the fern
Delicate movement of a furred
Fugitive creature hiding from the day.
Discovered secrets magnify his play
Into a vocation.

Laughing at education
He knows where the redshank hides her nest, perceives
a red-patch tremble when a coot lays seige
To water territory.
Nothing escapes his eye:
A ladybird
Slides like a blood-drop down a spear of grass;
The sapphire sparkle of a dragon-fly
Redeems a waste of weeds.
Collecting acorns, telling the beads of the year
On yew tree berries, his mind's too full for speech.

Back in the classroom he can never find
Answers to dusty questions, yet could teach,
Deeper than knowledge.
Geometry of twigs
Scratched on a sunlit wall;
History in stones,
Seasons told by the fields' calendar —
Living languages of Spring and Fall.

■ *Language and Concepts*

Alliteration
In poems the sound and the meaning should help each other.
When words which are close together have the same sounds,
particularly the same consonantal sound, this is called

alliteration, e.g. the 'forest's ferny floor', 'the silence surged softly backward'. Alliteration helps the music of the poem and also encourages us to connect similar sounding words together, thus creating new meaning.

■ *Readings and Responses*

1   Tell, in your own words, what this poem is about.

2   There are echoes of two nursery rhymes in the first verse. Can you detect them?

3   Pick out the two most evocative colour words in the poem.

4   Pick out some examples of alliteration.

5   School doesn't teach us the really important things in life. Prepare a speech for or against this motion.

The Best of School

D.H. Lawrence

The blinds are drawn because of the sun,
And the boys and the room in a colourless gloom
Of underwater float: bright ripples run
Across the walls as the blinds are blown
To let the sunlight in; and I,
As I sit on the shores of the class, alone,
Watch the boys in their summer blouses
As they write, their round heads busily bowed:
And one after another rouses
His face to look at me,
To ponder quietly,
As seeing, he does not see.

And then he turns again, with a little, glad
Thrill of his work he turns again from me,
Having found what he wanted, having got what was to be had.
And very sweet it is, while the sunlight waves
In the ripening morning, to sit alone with the class
And feel the stream of awakening ripple and pass

From me to the boys, whose brightening souls it laves
For this little hour.

            This morning, sweet it is
To feel the lads' looks light on me,
Then back in a swift, bright flutter to work:
Each one darting away with his
Discovery, like birds that steal and flee.
Touch after touch I feel on me

As their eyes glance at me for the grain
Of rigour they taste delightedly.
As tendrils reach out yearningly,
Slowly rotate till they touch the tree
That they cleave unto, and up which they climb
Up to their lives — so they to me.

I feel them cling and cleave to me
As vines going eagerly up; they twine
My life with other leaves, my time
Is hidden in theirs, their thrills are mine.

■ *Language and Concepts*

The ideal and the real
Human beings are very aware of the ideal — a state of perfection
when human desires are fulfilled. However, most people only
attain glimpses of the ideal and must be content with humdrum
reality.

■ *Readings and Responses*

1   Describe the scene and experience depicted in this poem.

2   Can you remember a class in which you were fully absorbed
    and which you thoroughly enjoyed? Describe it.

3   Would you say the picture painted in this poem is the ideal?
    Is the reality different?

4   Write a diary entry covering the events of yesterday at school.

5   How schools could be improved: my plan for Irish education.
    Prepare a talk or write an essay on this subject.

The Village Schoolmaster

Oliver Goldsmith

Beside yon straggling fence that skirts the way,
With blossom'd furze unprofitably gay,
There, in his noisy mansion, skilled to rule,
The village master taught his little school.
A man severe he was, and stern to view;
I knew him well, and every truant knew:
Well had the boding tremblers learned to trace
The day's disasters in his morning face;
Full well they laughed with counterfeited glee
At all his jokes, for many a joke had he;
Full well the busy whisper circling round
Conveyed the dismal tidings when he frowned.
Yet he was kind, or, if severe in aught,
The love he bore to learning was in fault;
The village all declared how much he knew:
'Twas certain he could write, and cypher too;
Lands he could measure, terms and tides presage,
And e'en the story ran that he could guage:
In arguing, too, the parson owned his skill;
For e'en though vanquished, he could argue still;
While words of learned length and thundering sound
Amazed the gazing rustics ranged around;
And still they gazed, and still the wonder grew,
That one small head could carry all he knew.

But past is all his fame. The very spot
Where many a time he triumphed, is forgot.

■ *Language and Concepts*

Rhyming Couplets
This is an extract from a long poem *The Deserted Village*, written
by Oliver Goldsmith in the eighteenth century. The poem is
written in rhyming couplets, i.e. each two lines rhyme.

■ *Readings and Responses*

1   Write a character sketch of the village schoolmaster.

2   Have teachers changed much in the last two hundred years?

3   Has society's attitude to teachers changed since then? Look
    particularly at the last eight lines.

4   Learn the first six lines by heart. Are rhyming couplets easier
    to learn by heart than poems without rhyme? Give reasons for
    your answer.

5   What is meant by the words 'The love he bore to learning'?

THREE ADVENTURE STORIES

■

The Bushrangers

The Shooting of Dan McGrew

Sir Patrick Spens

■

The Bushrangers

Edward Harrington

Four horsemen rode out from the heart of the range,
Four horsemen with aspects forbidding and strange.
They were booted and spurred, they were armed to the teeth,
And they frowned as they looked on the valley beneath,
As forward they rode through the rocks and the tern —

Ned Kelly, Dan Kelly, Steve Hart and Joe Byrne.
Ned Kelly drew rein and he shaded his eyes —
'The Town's at our mercy! See yonder it lies!
To hell with the troopers!' he shook his clenched fist —
'We will shoot them like dogs if they dare to resist!'
And all of them nodded, grim-visaged and stern —
Ned Kelly, Dan Kelly, Steve Hart and Joe Byrne.

Through the gullies and creeks they rode silently down;
They stuck-up the station and raided the town;
They opened the safe and they looted the bank;
They laughed and were merry, they ate and they drank.
Then off to the ranges they went with their gold —
Oh! never were bandits more reckless and bold.

But time brings its punishment, time travels fast —
And the outlaws were trapped in Glenrowan at last,
Where three of them died in the smoke and the flame,
And Ned Kelly came back — to the last he was game.
But the Law shot him down (he was fated to hang),
And that was the end of the bushranging gang.

Whatever their faults and whatever their crimes,
Their deeds lend romance to those faraway times.
They have gone from the gullies they haunted of old,
And nobody knows where they buried their gold.
To the ranges they loved they will never return —
Ned Kelly, Dan Kelly, Steve Hart and Joe Byrne.

But at times when I pass through that sleepy old town
Where the far-distant peaks of Strathbogie look down
I think of the days when those grim ranges rang
To the galloping hooves of the bushranging gang.
Though the years bring oblivion, time brings a change,
The ghosts of the Kellys still ride from the range.

Narrative poem
A narrative poem is a poem that tells a story. These poems are usually quite long because it is difficult to give the details of a story in a very short space.

■ *Readings and Responses*

1   Tell the story of Ned Kelly and his gang.

2   When you read the poem out loud what rhythm is suggested to your mind?

3   'Whatever their faults and whatever their crimes
    Their deeds lend romance to those faraway times.'

    What is meant by these lines? Do you think the 'crimes' of the gang were romantic? Would you think the phrase 'distance lends enchantment' applies here?

4   Look at the last verse. What comes to the poet's mind as he passes through the 'sleepy old town'?

5   Have you ever visited a place which seemed to contain ghosts of the past? Write a paragraph (or more) about it.

The Shooting of Dan McGrew

Robert Service

A bunch of the boys were whooping it up in the Malamute saloon;
The kid that handles the music-box was hitting a rag-time tune;
Back of the bar, in a solo game, sat Dangerous Dan McGrew,
And watching his luck was his light-o'-love, the lady that's known
    as Lou.

When out of the night, which was fifty below, and into the din
    and the glare,
There stumbled a miner fresh from the creeks, dog-dirty and
    loaded for bear.
He looked like a man with a foot in the grave, and scarcely the
    strength of a louse,
Yet he tilted a poke of dust on the bar, and he called for drinks
    for the house.
There was none could place the stranger's face, though we
    searched ourselves for a clue;
But we drank his health, and the last to drink was Dangerous
    Dan McGrew.

There's men that somehow just grip your eyes, and hold them
    hard like a spell;
And such was he, and he looked to me like a man who had lived
    in hell;
With a face most hair, and the dreary stare of a dog whose day is
    done,
As he watered the green stuff in his glass, and the drops fell one
    by one.
Then I got to figgering who he was, and wondering what he'd do
And I turned my head — and there watching him was the lady
    that's known as Lou.

His eyes went rubbering round the room, and he seemed in a
    kind of daze,
Till at last that old piano fell in the way of his wandering gaze.
The rag-time kid was having a drink; there was no one else on
    the stool,
So the stranger stumbles across the room and flops down there
    like a fool.
In a buckskin shirt that was glazed with dirt he sat, and I saw
    him sway;
Then he clutched the keys with his talon hands — my God! but
    that man could play!

Were you ever out in the Great Alone, when the moon was awful
    clear,

And the icy mountains hemmed you in with a silence you most
    could *hear*;
With only the howl of a timber wolf, and you camped there in the
    cold,
A half-dead thing in a stark, dead-world, clean mad for the muck
    called gold;
While high overhead, green, yellow, and red, the North Light
    swept in bars —
Then you've a hunch what the music meant ... hunger and night
    and the stars.

And hunger not of the belly kind, that's banished with bacon and
    beans;
But the gnawing hunger of lonely men for a home and all that it
    means;
For a fireside far from the cares that are, four walls and a roof
    above;
But oh! so cramful of cosy joy, and crowned with a woman's love:

A woman dearer than all the world, and true as Heaven is true —
(God! how ghastly she looks through her rouge — the lady that's
    known as Lou.)

Then on a sudden the music changed, so soft that you scarce
    could hear;
But you felt that your life had been looted clean of all that it once
    held dear;
That someone had stolen the woman you loved; that her love was
    a devil's lie;
That your guts were gone, and the best for you was to crawl away
    and die.
'Twas the crowning cry of a heart's despair, and it thrilled you
    through and through —
'I guess I'll make it a spread misere,' said Dangerous Dan
    McGrew.'

The music almost died away ... then it burst like a pent-up flood;
And it seemed to say, 'Repay, repay,' and my eyes were blind with
    blood.
The thought came back of an ancient wrong, and it stung like a
    frozen lash,
And the lust awoke to kill, to kill ... then the music stopped with
    a crash.

And the stranger turned, and his eyes they burned in a most
    peculiar way;
In a buckskin shirt that was glazed with dirt he sat, and I saw
    him sway;

Then his lips went in in a kind of grin, and he spoke, and his
   voice was calm;
And, 'Boys,' says he, 'you don't know me, and none of you care a
   damn;
But I want to state, and my words are straight, and I'll bet my
   poke they're true,
That one of you is a hound of hell ... and that one is Dan
   McGrew.

Then I ducked my head, and the lights went out, and two guns
   blazed in the dark;
And a woman screamed, and the lights went up, and two men lay
   stiff and stark.
Pitched on his head, and pumped full of lead, was Dangerous
   Dan McGrew.
While the man from the creeks lay clutched to the breast of the
   lady that's known as Lou.

These are the simple facts of the case, and I guess I ought to
   know;
They say that the stranger was crazed with 'hooch', and I'm not
   denying it's so.
I'm not so wise as the lawyer guys, but strictly between us two —
The woman that kissed him and — pinched his poke* — was the
   lady that's known as Lou.

* A poke is a bag

■ *Language and Concepts*

Recitation

In ancient Ireland the *reachtaire* used to recite the poems of the file
to an audience. Up to recent times many people used to learn a
'recitation' which they would recite as a party piece. The poems of
Robert Service are particularly popular as recitation pieces because
they tell a stirring story and they have a lively, bouncy rhythm.

■ *Readings and Responses*

1   What is the setting for this poem? Describe it as vividly as you
    can.

2   Look at the second and third verses. Describe the stranger
    who entered the saloon.

3   When the stranger began to play his music expressed 'hunger'.
    What kind of hunger? Look at the fifth and sixth verses.

4   What emotion is expressed by the music in verse seven?

5   Some people recite this poem as their 'party piece'. Why do
    you think it is suitable as a recitation?

Sir Patrick Spens

Anonymous

I The Sailing

The king sits in Dunfermline town
  Drinking the blude-red wine,
"O whare will I get a skeely skipper
  To sail this new ship o' mine?"

O up and spak an eldern knight,
  Sat at the king's right knee;
"Sir Patrick Spens is the best sailor
  That ever sailed the sea."

Our king has written a braid letter,
  And seal'd it with his hand,
And sent it to Sir Patrick Spens
  Was walking on the strand.

"To Noroway, to Noroway,
  To Noroway o'er the faem;
The king's daughter o' Noroway,
  'Tis thou must bring her hame."

The first word that Sir Patrick read
  So loud, loud laugh'd he;
The neist word that Sir Patrick read
  The tear blinded his e'e.

"O wha is this has done this deed
  And tauld the king o' me,
To send us out, at this time o' year,
  To sail upon the sea?

"Be it wind, be it weet, be it hail, be it sleet,
  Our ship must sail the faem;
The king's daughter o' Noroway,
  'Tis we must fetch her hame."

They hoysed their sails on Monenday morn
  Wi' a' the speed they may;
They hae landed in Noroway
  Upon a Wodensday.

II The Return

"Mak' ready, mak' ready, my merry men a'!
    Our gude ship sails the morn."
"Now ever alack, my master dear,
    I fear a deadly storm.

"I saw the new moon late yestreen
    Wi' the auld moon in her arm;
And if we gang to sea, master,
    I fear we'll come to harm."

They hadna sail'd a league, a league,
    A league but barely three,
When the lift grew dark, and the wind blew loud,
    And gurly grew the sea.

The ankers brak, and the topmast lap,
    It was sic a deadly storm:
And the waves cam owre the broken ship
    Till a' her sides were torn.

"Go fetch a web o' the silken claith,
    Another o' the twine,
And wap them into our ship's side,
    And let nae the sea come in."

They fetch'd a web o' the silken claith,
    Another o' the twine,
And they wapp'd them round that gude ship's side,
    But still the sea cam in.

O laith, laith were our gude Scots lords
    To wet their cork-heel'd shoon;
But lang or a' the play was play'd
    They wat their hats aboon.

And mony was the feather bed
    That flatter'd on the faem;
And mony was the gude lord's son
    That never mair cam hame.

O lang, lang may the ladies sit,
    Wi' their fans into their hand,
Before they see Sir Patrick Spens
    Come sailing to the strand!

And lang, lang may the maidens sit
    Wi' their gowd kames in their hair,

> A-waiting for their ain dear loves!
>   For them they'll see nae mair.
>
> Half-owre, half-owre to Aberdour,
>   'Tis fifty fathoms deep;
> And there lies gude Sir Patrick Spens,
>   Wi' the Scots lórds at his feet!

■ *Language and Concepts*

Traditional ballad
Traditional ballads are songs of unknown authorship passed down orally from generation to generation. See page 65 for the characteristics of the ballad.

■ *Readings and Responses*

1   Tell in your own words the story of this poem.

2   Did Sir Patrick have a premonition that something tragic might happen? Support your answer by referring to the poem.

3   'And gurly grew the sea'. 'Gurly' is a Scots dialect word. What do you think it means? Look at the context before you answer. Do you think it is an evocative word?

4   Is there a hint of satire in the second last, third last and fifth last verses? What does this suggest about the unknown author of the ballad?

5   How many aspects of the ballad form can you find in this poem?

EAVAN BOLAND

Eavan Boland was born in Dublin in 1944. Her father was a diplomat so she lived abroad for some time. She now lives in Dublin with her husband, the novelist Kevin Casey, and her two daughters.

Eavan Boland has stated that her desire is 'to bless the ordinary ... sanctify the common'. What she means by this is that we must deal with our ordinary day-to-day lives and see the value in our ordinary activities. Her poems also display great imaginative insight and precision and exactness of language.

Night Feed

It's a Woman's World

Patchwork

The Black Lace Fan my Mother Gave me

The War Horse

Hymn

Night Feed

Eavan Boland

This is dawn.
Believe me
This is your season, little daughter.
The moment daisies open,
The hour mercurial rainwater
Makes a mirror for sparrows.
It's time we drowned our sorrows.

I tiptoe in.
I lift you up
Wriggling
In your rosy, zipped sleeper.
Yes, this is the hour
For the early bird and me
When finder is keeper.

I crook the bottle.
How you suckle!
This is the best I can be,
Housewife
To this nursery
Where you hold on,
Dear life.

A silt of milk
The last suck.
And now your eyes are open,
Birth-coloured and offended.
Earth wakes.
You go back to sleep.
The feed is ended.

Worms turn
Stars go in.
Even the moon is losing face.
Poplars stilt for dawn
And we begin
The long fall from grace.
I tuck you in.

■ *Readings and Responses*

1   The poet presents us with a scene. What scene is this? In
    your answer refer to the time of day, the quietness and
    nature.

2   What very ordinary activity does the poet invest with great importance in this poem? Look at the words 'Dear life' as part of your answer.

3   Describe the baby's appearance. Refer to the precise words used by the poet.

4   What does the poet mean by the words 'This is the best I can be'?

5   Feeding the baby is invested with great importance. What line in the last verse suggests that the remainder of life will involve problems?

It's a Woman's World

Eavan Boland

Our way of life
has hardly changed
since a wheel first
whetted a knife.

Maybe flame
burns more greedily
and wheels are steadier,
but we're the same:

we milestone
our lives
with oversights,
living by the lights
of the loaf left

by the cash register,
the washing powder
paid for and wrapped,
the wash left wet:

like most historic peoples
we are defined
by what we forget

and what we never will be:
star-gazers,
fire-eaters.
It's our alibi
for all time:

as far as history goes
we were never
on the scene of the crime.

When the king's head
gored its basket,
grim harvest,
we were gristing bread

or getting the recipe
for a good soup.
It's still the same:

our windows
moth our children

to the flame
of hearth not history.

And still no page
scores the low music
of our outrage.

Appearances reassure:
that woman there,
craned to
the starry mystery,

is merely getting a breath
of evening air.
While this one here,
her mouth a burning plume —

she's no fire-eater,
just my frosty neighbour
coming home.

■ *Language and Concepts*

Symbol
When a word is used to refer not only to itself but is meant to
stand for something else, it is a symbol. The Cross is the symbol
of Christianity, the dove is the symbol of peace.

What are the following words symbols for?
a fox, a lion, a white flag, black.

■ *Readings and Responses*

1   This is a poem which suggests that the role of women has
    been overlooked throughout history. Where in the poem is it
    suggested that women are so busy that they forget things?

2   In the fifth verse it is stated that women will never be 'star-
    gazers' or 'fire-eaters'. What are these two words symbols for?

3   Why, according to the poet, were women not present at the
    great moments of history?

4   Quote the lines which suggest that women are upset that
    their role is not recognised.

5   Are the women in the last three verses really 'star-gazers' and
    'fire-eaters'?

Patchwork

Eavan Boland

I have been thinking at random
on the universe,
or rather, how nothing in the universe
is random —
(there's nothing like presumption late at night.)

My sumptuous
trash bag of colours —
Laura Ashley cottons —
waits to be cut
and stitched and patched but

there's a mechanical feel
about the handle
of my second-hand sewing machine,
with its flowers,
and 'Singer' painted orange,
and its iron wheel.

My back is to the dark.
Somewhere out there
are stars and bits of stars,
and little bits of bits,
and swiftnesses and brightnesses and drift —
but is it craft or art?

I will be here

till midnight,
cross-legged in the dining room,
logging triangles and diamonds,
cutting and aligning,
finding greens in pinks
and burgundies in white
until I finish it.

There's no reason in it.

Only when it's laid
right across the floor —
sphere on sphere
and seam on seam
in a good light —
will it start to hit me:

these are not bits
they are pieces
and the pieces fit.

1 Describe in words or by drawing or painting, the picture created by the poet.

2 What do all the little bits of material remind the poet of? Remember she had been thinking of the universe.

3 What is meant by the statement 'nothing in the universe is random'?

4 It is suggested in the last verse that there is a difference between 'bits' and 'pieces'. What is this difference?

5 In what way is the completed patchwork quilt like the sky?

The Black Lace Fan my Mother Gave me

Eavan Boland

It was the first gift he ever gave her,
buying it for five francs in the Galeries
in pre-war Paris. It was stifling.
A starless drought made the nights stormy.

They stayed in the city for the summer.
They met in cafés. She was always early.
He was late. That evening he was later.
They wrapped the fan. He looked at his watch.

She looked down the Boulevard des Capucines.
She ordered more coffee. She stood up.
The streets were emptying. The heat was killing.
She thought the distance smelled of rain and lightning.

These are wild roses, appliqued on silk by hand,
darkly picked, stitched boldly, quickly.
The rest is tortoiseshell and has the reticent,
clear patience of its element. It is

a worn-out, underwater bullion and it keeps,
even now, an inference of its violation.
The lace is overcast as if the weather
it opened for and offset had entered it.

The past is an empty café terrace.
An airless dusk before thunder. A man running.
And no way now to know what happened then —
none at all — unless, of course, you improvise:

The blackbird on this first sultry morning,
in summer, finding buds, worms, fruit,
feels the heat. Suddenly she puts out her wing —
the whole, full, flirtatious span of it.

■ *Readings and Responses*

1   Describe what happened in the café in pre-war Paris.

2   What stimulates the poet to think about that night in Paris?

3   Try to describe the fan in your own words.

4   Do you possess any object, such as a penknife or a
    photograph, perhaps, which possesses particular meaning for
    you? Write a paragraph (or more) about it.

5   Look at the last verse carefully. In what sense is the blackbird
    like the fan? What word suggests the beginning of a love-
    affair?

The War Horse

Eavan Boland

This dry night, nothing unusual
About the clip, clop, casual

Iron of his shoes as he stamps death
Like a mint on the innocent coinage of earth.

I lift the window, watch the ambling feather
Of hock and fetlock, loosed from its daily tether

In the tinker camp on the Enniskerry Road,
Pass, his breath hissing, his snuffling head

Down. He is gone. No great harm is done.
Only a leaf of our laurel hedge is torn —

Of distant interest like a maimed limb,
Only a rose which now will never climb

The stone of our house, expendable, a mere
Line of defence against him, a volunteer

You might say, only a crocus its bulbous head
Blown from growth, one of the screamless dead.

But we, we are safe, our unformed fear
Of fierce commitment gone; why should we care

If a rose, a hedge, a crocus are uprooted
Like corpses, remote, crushed, mutilated?

He stumbles on like a rumour of war, huge,
Threatening; neighbours use the subterfuge

Of curtains; he stumbled down our short street
Thankfully passing us. I pause, wait,

Then to breathe relief lean on the sill
And for a second only my blood is still

With atavism. That rose he smashed frays
Ribboned across our hedge, recalling days

Of burned countryside, illicit braid:
A cause ruined before, a world betrayed.

Literal/symbolic
The literal meaning of a word or a sentence is its normal, everyday meaning — the meaning that might be given in a dictionary. If a word or sentence has a symbolic meaning, it will refer to something other than its surface meaning. In the poem above, the word 'horse' has a literal and a symbolic level of meaning.

■ *Readings and Responses*

1   Tell the literal story of this poem.

2   What word in the third line suggests that the horse represents something fearful.

3   The horse destroys a leaf of the laurel hedge, a rose and a crocus. What words suggest that there is an underlying meaning to the horse's destruction?

4   In the last five lines the poet is reminded of times of rebellion and revenge in Ireland. What words suggest this?

5   Is there a nightmare quality about this poem? How is this atmosphere built up?

Hymn

Eavan Boland

Four a.m.
December.
A lamb would perish
out there.

The cutlery glitter
of that sky
has nothing in it
I want to follow.

Here is the star
of my nativity:
the nursery lamp
in that suburb window,

behind which
is boiled glass, a bottle,
and a baby all
hissing like a kettle.

The light goes out.
The blackbird
takes up his part.
I wake by habit.
I know it all by heart:

these candles
and the altar
and the psaltery of dawn.

And in the dark
as we slept
the world
was made flesh.

■ *Readings and Responses*

1 What are the nuances in the word 'cutlery' in verse two?

2 What replaces the star of Bethlehem for the poet?

3 It is suggested in the last verse that Christ was born
overnight. Where is this suggested?

4 Write a short paragraph describing the sky on a starry night.

5 Is the poet hinting that we can serve God by looking after our
own families? Remember that the poem is entitled *Hymn.*

ALL YOU NEED IS LOVE?

Poetry can be about anything! The poet Wordsworth said that nothing human was alien to him. However, most poetry deals with the major matters of human existence: love, death, suffering, joy, fear. 'Love', in all its varieties, is such a profound emotion that many people feel that only in poetry can it be, in some sense, understood. When you have read some of the poems in this section, pick out your favourite love-poem.

I know where I'm going

Growing Pain

Medicine

Day of these Days

A Frosty Night

The Man Who Never Had A Visitor

'As I walked out one evening'

The Passionate Shepherd to His Love

She Dwelt Among the Untrodden Ways

I know where I'm going

Anonymous

I know where I'm going,
I know who's going with me,
I know who I love,
But the dear knows who I'll marry.

I'll have stockings of silk
Shoes of fine green leather,
Combs to buckle my hair
And a ring for every finger.

Feather beds are soft,
Painted rooms are bonny;
But I'd leave them all
To go with my love Johnny.

Some say he's dark,
I say he's bonny,
He's the flower of them all
My handsome, winsome Johnny.

I know where I'm going,
I know who's going with me,
I know who I love,
But the dear knows who I'll marry.

■ *Language and Concepts*

Song and lyric
A song contains words that are meant to be sung. A lyric poem is a short poem which expresses a person's own feelings in rhythmic language. It may or may not be sung.

■ *Readings and Responses*

1   How would you describe the mood of this love-song?

2   Are there romantic aspects to this poem? Pick out the words and images which are romantic.

3   How does the singer show that her love for Johnny is the most important thing in the world for her?

4   Many popular songs are love-songs. Collect the words of some of these love-songs and decide which contains the most powerful words.

5   Does the girl in this song have any doubts about her love for Johnny?

Growing Pain

Vernon Scannell

The boy was barely five years old.
We sent him to the little school
And left him there to learn the names
Of flowers in jam jars on the sill
And learn to do as he was told.
He seemed quite happy there until
Three weeks afterwards, at night,
The darkness whimpered in his room.
I went upstairs, switched on his light,
And found him wide awake, distraught,
Sheets mangled and his eiderdown
Untidy carpet on the floor.
I said, 'Why can't you sleep? A pain?'
He snuffled, gave a little moan,
And then he spoke a single word
'Jessica' The sound was blurred
'Jessica? What do you mean?'
'A girl at school called Jessica,
She hurts' — he touched himself between
The heart and stomach — 'she has been
Aching here and I can see her.'
Nothing I had read or heard
Instructed me in what to do.
I covered him and stroked his head
'The pain will go, in time,' I said.

■ *Readings and Responses*

1   Why can't the little boy sleep?

2   Why does the father find it almost impossible to cope with the situation?

3   'The pain will go, in time.' What does this tell us about the father?

4   Children's feelings can be just as deep and profound as those of much older people. Is this true?

5   What lines show us that the young boy hasn't the language to cope with his feelings?

Medicine

Alice Walker

Grandma sleeps with
my sick
   grand-
pa so she
can get him
during the night
medicine
to stop
   the pain

   In
the morning
clumsily
   I
wake
   them

Her eyes
look at me
from under-
      neath
his withered
arm

   The
medicine
   is all
   in
her long
   un-
      braided
      hair.

■ *Readings and Responses*

1   Is this a love-poem? How is it different from the usual love-poems?

2   This poem could be said to describe a very poignant situation. What is meant by 'poignant'?

3   Is the word 'withered' a good word?

4   What is meant by the last sentence? Does the way it is printed, with only part of a word or one or two words in each line, suggest anything?

Day of these Days

Laurie Lee

Such a morning it is when love
leans through geranium windows
and calls with a cockerel's tongue.

When red-haired girls scamper like roses
over the rain-green grass,
and the sun drips honey.

When hedgerows grow venerable,
berries dry black as blood,
and holes suck in their bees.

Such a morning it is when mice
run whispering from the church,
dragging dropped ears of harvest.

When the partridge draws back his spring
and shoots like a buzzing arrow
over grained and mahogany fields.

When no table is bare
and no bread dry
and the tramp feeds off ribs of rabbit.

Such a day it is when time
piles up the hills like pumpkins
and the streams run golden.

When all men smell good,
and the cheeks of girls
are as baked bread to the mouth.

As bread and bean flowers
the touch of their lips,
and their white teeth sweeter than cucumbers.

■ *Language and Concepts*

Pathetic fallacy
When nature is thought to be in harmony with our feelings this is
called pathetic fallacy. If we are very sad and it begins to rain,
nature would be in harmony with our feelings. But it is a fallacy
(false reasoning) to believe that the rain began so as to be in
harmony with our feeling.

1 'I smell blossoms but the trees are bare
   I hear singing but there's no one there.
   All day long I seem to walk on air.
   I wonder why, I wonder why.'
   People in the first flush of romantic love are said to see the
   world in a new fresh way; everything seems to have a new
   shine. In *Day of these Days*, life seems beautiful and
   wonderful. Pick out your two favourite examples of this in the
   poem.

2 Pick out examples of the appeal to each of the five senses.

3 Pick out the utopian images of plenty.

4 What metaphor is used in verse five?

5 Try to write some lines in the style of verse six.

A Frosty Night

Robert Graves

'Alice, dear, what ails you,
    Dazed and lost and shaken?
Has the chill night numbed you?
    Is it fright you have taken?'

'Mother, I am very well,
    I was never better.
Mother, do not hold me so,
    Let me write my letter.'

'Sweet, my dear, what ails you?'
    'No, but I am well.
The night was cold and frosty —
    There's no more to tell.'

'Ay, the night was frosty,
    Coldly gaped the moon,
Yet the birds seemed twittering
    Through green boughs of June.

'Soft and thick the snow lay,
    Stars danced in the sky —
Not all the lambs of May-day
    Skip so bold and high.

'Your feet were dancing, Alice
        Seemed to dance on air,
You looked a ghost or angel
        In the star-light there.

'Your eyes were frosted star-light;
        Your heart, fire and snow,
Who was it said, "I love you"?'
        'Mother, let me go!'

■ *Language and Concepts*

The Ballad
The ballad is a type of poem. To be a ballad it should have most of the following characteristics:

(a) One single story or idea

(b) Much repetition giving an incantatory effect

(c) Each verse has four lines with a rhyming scheme usually ABCB

(d) Heavy rhythmic beat

(e) Question and answer format

(f) A climax is reached without any comment from the narrator.

■ *Readings and Responses*

1 Who are the two people talking in this poem? Work out precisely who says what.

2 The mother suspects that Alice is in love. Who is speaking in verses four, five and six? Has the mother knowledge of how a person in love feels?

3 Why does Alice not want to talk about her feelings?

4 People in the first flush of love are said to see the world as having a new shine. Where is this feeling suggested in this poem?

5 Pick out the characteristics of the ballad present in this poem.

The Man Who Never Had A Visitor

Michael D. Higgins

They all knew about him
But nobody ever spoke
To the man who never had a visitor
In St Teresa's Ward
He had come so long ago
Nobody could remember.

It was the neighbours who brought him in
They heard,
On a strange night,
Of a high tide.

He spoke occasionally to the bushes
Or arranging the flowers in vases
He would be heard to whisper
But I know, I know
Why I did it.

In the village the story was well known
Of the man who burned his wife's house
Together they'd lived for thirty years
Without benefit of chick nor child
But he would look at her
In a slow way that they both knew
Was love in a time when softness was not allowed.
And the day he found her
Stretched in front of the fire
The tongs grasped in her hand
He screamed and ran from the house.

It was poitín that made the funeral pass
The neighbours shovelled out the clay
From his mother's grave
And one dead lover met another
And it was poitín too that did it,
They said.

When weeping in the corner of the bar
He could take it no more
And never returned home.

The priest, a young man, came
And brought him home
Pull yourself together Colie, he said
Life must go on

But all he could see was the dresser
And the two plates where she left them
And the two mugs
And the two chairs

There was two of everything
There will be one of nothing,
He screamed
And ran outside
The Man whose lover had died
And coming back
He brought a can
Asking the priest to come outside,
He cast the petrol at the gable thatch
And as his house burned he fell to his knees
And tears came
And he shook and screamed
They said it was the poitín
but all he said was
I will not let it be.
There was two of everything
There will be one of nothing.

And the neighbours saw the flames
Of the house of the man
Whose lover was gone.
My God, they said, he must be mad
To burn his cosy little house.
And they brought him here
On a strange night,
Of a high tide. And
They all knew about him
But nobody ever spoke
To the man who never had a visitor
In St Teresa's ward.
He had come so long ago
Nobody could remember.

And in the village they didn't speak
Of the terrible things
That happened on a strange night
Of a high tide
When a man went mad
And burned his house

Screaming only
There was two of everything
There will be one of nothing.

There were many things better
Left unsaid
And some poor people best
Forgotten.

■ *Language and concepts*

The refrain
Sometimes in a poem a line or lines are repeated regularly rather
like a chorus in a song; these lines are called the refrain. The
refrain should provide the key to the theme of the poem.

■ *Readings and Responses*

1   Tell the story related in this poem.

2   What is meant by 'in a time when softness was not allowed'.
    Is 'softness' allowed nowadays?

3   What is meant by
        'There was two of everything
        There will be one of nothing'?
    How many times in the poem are these lines repeated? Are
    they a kind of refrain?

4   Is this a poem about love or loneliness or both?

5   What is meant by the last two lines?

'As I walked out one evening'

W.H. Auden

As I walked out one evening,
    Walking down Bristol Street,
The crowds upon the pavement
    Were fields of harvest wheat.

And down by the brimming river
    I heard a lover sing
Under an arch of the railway:
    'Love has no ending.

'I'll love you, dear, I'll love you
    Till China and Africa meet,
And the river jumps over the mountain
    And the salmon sing in the street,

'I'll love you till the ocean
    Is folded and hung up to dry
And the seven stars go squawking
    Like geese about the sky.

'The years shall run like rabbits,
    For in my arms I hold
The Flower of the Ages,
    And the first love of the world.'

But all the clocks in the city
    Began to whirr and chime:
'O let not Time deceive you,
    You cannot conquer Time.

'In the burrows of the Nightmare
    Where Justice naked is,
Time watches from the shadow
    And coughs when you would kiss.

'In headaches and in worry
    Vaguely life leaks away,
And Time will have his fancy
    Tomorrow or today.

'Into many a green valley
    Drifts the appalling snow;
Time breaks the threaded dances
    And the diver's brilliant bow.

'O plunge your hands in water,
    Plunge them in up to the wrist;

Stare, stare in the basin
   And wonder what you've missed.

'The glacier knocks in the cupboard,
   The desert sighs in the bed,
And the crack in the tea-cup opens
   A lane to the land of the dead.

'Where the beggars raffle the banknotes
   And the Giant is enchanting to Jack,
And the lily-white Boy is a Roarer,
   And Jill goes down on her back.

'O look, look in the mirror,
   O Look in your distress;
Life remains a blessing
   Although you cannot bless.

'O stand, stand at the window
   As the tears scald and start;
You shall love your crooked neighbour
   With your crooked heart.'

It was late, late in the evening,
   The lovers they were gone;
The clocks had ceased their chiming
   And the deep river ran on.

◼ *Language and Concepts*

Hyperbole
Hyperbole is the use of exaggeration in order to create an effect or emphasise a point, e.g. 'I'd walk a million miles for one of your smiles.'

◼ *Readings and Responses*

1   In this poem there are two speakers. Who are they? Work out in general terms what they both say.

2   Pick out the examples of hyperbole in verses three and four. Why is there so much hyperbole in poems dealing with love?

3   What is meant by the lines:
'Time watches from the shadow
And coughs when you would kiss'.

4   What view of life is presented in verses eight and ten?

5   What is meant by the images in verse eleven?

6   What characteristics of the ballad are present in this poem?

The Passionate Shepherd to His Love

Christopher Marlowe

Come live with me and be my Love,
And we will all the pleasures prove
That valleys, groves, hills, and fields,
Woods or steepy mountains yields.

And we will sit upon the rocks
Seeing the shepherds feed their flocks,
By shallow rivers, to whose falls
Melodious birds sing madrigals.

And I will make thee beds of roses
And a thousand fragrant posies,
A cap of flowers, and a kirtle
Embroidered all with leaves of myrtle;

A gown made of the finest wool,
Which from our pretty lambs we pull;
Fair lined slippers for the cold,
With buckles of the purest gold;

A belt of straw and ivy buds
With coral clasps and amber studs;
And if these pleasures may thee move,
Come live with me and be my Love.

The shepherd swains shall dance and sing
For thy delight each May morning:
If these delights thy mind may move,
Then live with me and be my Love.

■ *Language and Concepts*

Convention

In behaviour, 'convention' means the commonly accepted way of behaving; in literature a convention is a commonly accepted, traditional way of presenting an idea. *The Passionate Shepherd to His Love* is a poem written within a convention — the pastoral love poem. In this convention, the poet imagines that he and his loved one will live idyllic lives as shepherds.

■ *Readings and Responses*

1   Does this poem share the hyperbole common to love poems? Pick out two examples.

2   Look at the rhyming couplets.

3   Do you think the poet is sincere?

4   Describe the idyllic life the lovers will lead.

She Dwelt Among the Untrodden Ways

William Wordsworth

She dwelt among the untrodden ways
    Beside the springs of Dove,
A maid whom there were none to praise
    And very few to love:

A violet by a mossy stone
    Half hidden from the eye!
— Fair as a star, when only one
    Is shining in the sky.

She lived unknown, and few could know
    When Lucy ceased to be:
But she is in her grave, and, oh,
    The difference to me!

■ *Language and Concepts*

Monosyllabic and polysyllabic words
Monosyllabic words are words of one syllable. Polysyllabic words
are words of many syllables. We tend to use monosyllabic words
to express deep, immediate emotions or concerns. If a person is
drowning they are more likely to shout the monosyllabic word
'help' than the polysyllabic, 'render me assistance'.

■ *Readings and Responses*

1   Are the words in this poem monosyllabic or polysyllabic? Why
are the words suitable for the emotion being expressed?

2   What are we told about Lucy herself?

3   What images are used in the second verse to describe Lucy?
What do they tell us about her?

4   What is the effect of the word 'oh' in line eleven?

5   We don't know who Lucy was except that she lives near the
river Dove. Try to imaginatively create a portrait of her life.

MICHAEL COADY

■

Michael Coady was born in 1939 in Carrick-on-Suir, Co. Tipperary where he still lives and works as a teacher. In 1981 he received a bursary from The Arts Council of Ireland which enabled him to travel in the U.S.A.

Job Wilks and the River

The Letter

Asembling the Parts

Newborn Feet

The Invisible Hotel

■

Job Wilks and the River

Michael Coady

*'...of the 56th Regiment, who died accidentally by drowning, at
Carrick-on-Suir, 17th July 1868, in his 28th year.'*

I feel that I know you, Job Wilks —

no imperial trooper swaggering
these servile Tipperary streets
before my grandfather drew breath,
but a country lad out of Hardy,
drunk on payday and pining for Wessex,
flirting with Carrick girls
in fetid laneways after dark,

out of step on parade to Sunday Service
with comrades who loved you enough
to raise out of soldiers' pay this stone
which would halt my feet among nettles
now that jackdaws are free in the chancel,
Communion plate lies deep
in the dark of a bank vault,
and spinster daughter of the last
rector, in a home for the aged,
whispers all night to an only brother
dead these forty years in Burma.

How commonplace, Job Wilks, how strange
that this should be where
it would end for you, twenty-eight
summers after the midwife washed you.
With that first immersion
you took your part
in the music of what happens,
and an Irish river was flowing
to meet you, make you
intimate clay of my town.

On a July day of imperial sun
did your deluged eyes find
vision of Wessex, as Suir water
sang in your brain?

I know the same river you knew, Job,
the same sky and hill and stone bridge:
I hope there were Carrick girls with tears
for a country lad out of Hardy,
drunk on payday and pining
for Wessex.

1   Job Wilks didn't 'swagger'. According to the first eleven lines, what kind of person was he?

2   What is suggested by the words, 'twenty-eight/summers after the midwife washed you'?

3   'you took your part/in the music of what happens'. Do these lines say something about all humanity?

4   What is meant by the lines, 'as Suir water/sang in your brain'?

5   What hope does the poet express in the last four lines?

The Letter

for James Coady, lost father of my grandfather

Michael Coady

1

If there can be some
redemption in the word
then let this telling reach
across the silence
of a hundred years
In Oven Lane.

About your feet upon the earthen floor
let me find the child who will
out of the slow unravelling
become my grandfather
and in the curtained room
your young wife Mary Eager
still beside an infant
bound with her in rituals
of laying-out and prayer.

This dark hour's nativity
will shape and scar your destiny
and in the unformed future
cast its shadow over hearts
that will engender me;
in time it will call up
this impulse
and these words.

Let me try to know you
in the anguish of that hour

a man of no importance
trapped in a narrow place,
enmeshed in desperate circumstance
as at the whim of some
malignant puppeteer.

The image holds the lane,
its stench, the fetid hovels
crowding down toward
the quayside of the Suir
where kinship and compassion
resurrect in time upon the page
the murmured solidarity
and flickering of candles
about the human face
of piteous travail.

2
A hundred years and I will come
to try the lane for echoes
the coughing and the crying
of children in the dark,
the nameless incarnations
of love and grief and hunger
where the river flows
coldly past.

These broken walls were witness
to your leaving, whether
in morning sun or rain,
your firstborn child still sleeping
when you left him,
the dark-shawled blessings
from the doorways of a lane
you'd never see again.

3
What I know has come to me
out of dead mouths:
through the barefoot child
left with your father,
the old boatman, and from
the mouth of my own father,
that child's son.

A life I'll never know
is buried with you
in a place
I'll never find:

a generation turned before
the morning of the letter
sent to find your son
become a man
with children of his own.

Out of the maze of circumstance,
the ravelled tangle of effect and cause,
something impelled you,
brought you finally
to bend above
the unmarked page —

an old man
in some room in Philadelphia
reaching for words to bridge
the ocean of his silence,
pleading forgiveness of the child
of Oven Lane.

4
Silence was the bitter
answer you were given
every empty day
until you died:

by a breakfast table
my child father
watched your son unseal
his darkest pain

saw the pages torn and cast
in mortal grief and anger
out of an abandoned child's
unspeakable heart-hunger
into the brute finality
of flame.

5
Now all of these
have gone into the dark
and I would try again
to reconcile the hearts

of which my heart's compounded
with words upon a page.

I send this telling out
to meet the ghosts
of its begetting
to release it from stone mouths
of Oven Lane.

■ *Readings and Responses*

1   The story told in this wonderful poem is quite complicated.
    Try to unravel the sequence of events and then tell the story
    in your own words.

2   The poet tries to find some reasons why his great- grandfather
    might have left. Look at the last fifteen lines of section 1 of the
    poem and say why you think he left.

3   Why did the great-grandfather finally write 'the letter'? See
    section 3.

4   Why was the letter thrown in the fire? See section 4.

5   Would you call this a tragic story? Does the poet manage to
    understand everyone's motives? What does this poem tell us
    about human nature?

Assembling the Parts

Michael Coady

Standing in sunshine
by Highway 84
I'm photographing a factory
which is no longer there

looking for my father
by an assembly line
which has halted
and vanished into air

catching the sepia ghost
of a young tubercular Irishman
who's left a rooming house
at 6 a.m. in a winter time
during the Depression

when my mother is still a girl
playing precocious violin,
a Miraculous Medal under
her blouse, in Protestant
oratorios in Waterford.

A pallid face in the crowd
in a dark winter time,
he's coughing in the cold,
assembling typewriters
in Hartford, Connecticut,

waiting for blood on his pillow
to send him home, where he'll
meet her one ordinary
night with the band playing
Solitude in the Foresters' Hall.

Fifty years on
he's nine Septembers dead
and a tourist in sunshine
by Highway 84
is photographing a factory
which is no longer there,

assembling the parts
of the mundane mystery,
the common enigma of journeys
and unscheduled destinations,

the lost intersections
of person and place and time
uniquely fathering everyman
out of the random dark.

■ *Readings and Responses*

1   Tell the story of the poet's father's life as it is told in the poem.

2   Look up the word 'sepia' in the dictionary. In what context is
    the word 'sepia' usually used?

3   The poet's father and mother would not have met but for
    something happening to the father. What does this tell us
    about life in general?

4   The words 'mystery', 'enigma' and 'random' are used in the
    last two verses. What do these words suggest about people's
    lives?

5   What is meant by the title of the poem?

Newborn Feet

Michael Coady

Toward what rooms,
what doors and windows
will those unshod feet bear you?
There are things preparing —

there are others, born
or to be made, and they
will come to meet you
in the mystery of faring

toward unknown destinations
found by choice and chance
along unfolding paths
of questing and creating.

■ *Language and Concepts*

Connotations
The connotations of a word are all the ideas, emotions and
pictures conjured up in our minds by that word, e.g. the word
'vicious' might have connotations of cruelty; it might bring to
mind images of a fierce dog; it might provoke fear, and so on.
What are the connotations of these words: lamb; sea; yellow;
daffodil; proud?

■ *Readings and Responses*

1   To whom do you think this poem might be addressed?

2   What is suggested about life by the use of the words 'mystery'
and 'unknown'?

3   The poem seems to suggest that life is governed by 'choice
and chance'. Explain what is meant by this.

4   Life also involves 'questing and creating'. Explain.

5   'Newborn feet' and 'unshod feet' are mentioned. What
connotations do these words bring to your mind?

The Invisible Hotel

Michael Coady

Stand at the turn and see quite clearly
Kennedy's Hotel no longer there; hold
in the eye this void where everything
ordinary happened in its time

and slow-dissolved into a clarified
intrigue of space now absolutely innocent
of every brick and wall and window, with all
of maids and cattle-jobbers, drinkers and cardplayers,
shoes and sheets and knives and pots and basins,
plates and dinners and the creaking stair
recycled utterly to air.

Flesh out the inventory with snores and singing,
boiled potatoes and the aftersmell of cabbage,
copulation, defecation and death-rattle,
glint of glass and amber eye of whiskey,
melodeons and chamber pots and sides of bacon,
fires alight and rain against the windows,
steam and coins and candles and
the grey rewind of mornings after.

Pick a card from out the shuffled
and reshuffled deck
of darkened instances —

the starched cuffs of Francesco Marchetti
come to sell beads and prayer books
from a booth during the Parish Mission
taking lamb's liver with his tea and all
unguessing that after sermon and Benediction
he'll meet his force of destiny in Mary Browne
who's still demurely cutting calico
upstairs under gaslight in the drapery
of P.Bourke & Co., Main Street,
or from the voided clamour and the whispering
choose the gone-to-silence scales and trills
of beautiful Miss Olive Westwood warming up
with Maestro Albert Bowyer on pianoforte
to give her golden arias above a trance of faces
in the Town Hall for that night only,
while in the dark backyard Liz Callaghan
is tipping slops to pigs
that fatten for the winter.

There, as clear as day,
it all no longer is
from where you're passing
between Town Wall and Lough Street,
under the salmon on the Town Clock
turning in the wind to spawn
each day's conspiring weather.

 Language and Concepts

Paradox
A paradox is a statement which on first reading seems false but
on further reflection is seen to contain a truth. The first two lines
of this poem contain a paradox. On first reading it seems
nonsensical to be able to 'see quite clearly' something which isn't
there. Further reflection, however, shows us that we can see the
hotel and all its activities quite clearly in our imaginations.

 Readings and Responses

1   There is a wonderful picture of turbulent life as it was in the
    no longer existing hotel. Does the poet cover nearly all aspects
    of human life?

2   What is the poet suggesting when he speaks of life as similar
    to being dealt a hand of cards?

3   Tell the story of Francesco and Mary.

4   The lifestyles of two contrasted women are presented in verse
    six. What are they?

5   Explain the paradox in the lines

    'There, as clear as day,
    it all no longer is'.

FAMILY LIFE — LIVING WITH OTHERS

■

Most people live much of their lives within families. The values we absorb, the emotions we feel, the experiences we have, leave a deep impression in our minds. The following six poems reflect the importance of family life. Other poems on family life in this book are *Nightfeed* by Eavan Boland, *Stellar Manipulator* by Paul Durcan, *The Letter* by Michael Coady and *Silver Flask* by John Montague.

Nettles

My Gramp

To Lauren Newly Born

Power Cut

Watching My Father Shaving

The Inter

■

Nettles

Vernon Scannell

My son aged three fell in the nettle bed.
'Bed' seemed a curious name for those green spears,
That regiment of spite behind the shed:
It was no place for rest. With sobs and tears
The boy came seeking comfort and I saw
White blisters beaded on his tender skin.
We soothed him till his pain was not so raw.
At last he offered us a watery grin,
And then I took my billhook, honed the blade
And went outside and slashed in fury with it
Till not a nettle in that fierce parade
Stood upright anymore. And then I lit
A funeral pyre to burn the fallen dead
But in two weeks the busy sun and rain
Had called up tall recruits behind the shed:
My son would often feel sharp wounds again.

■ *Language and Concepts*

Visual image
When a writer, by his careful choice of words, creates a picture
which you can see, this is called a visual image.

■ *Readings and Responses*

1   What is the moral or message contained in this poem?

2   Pick out all the words in this poem which have some
connection with armies. Why are there so many such words?

3   'White blisters beaded on his tender skin.'

Discuss this image.

4   What is conveyed by the use of the word 'watery' in 'watery
grin'?

5   Write a description of the worst pain you experienced as a
child. Search for the right words to describe the pain.

My Gramp

Derek Stuart

My gramp has got a medal.
On the front there is a runner.
On the back it says:
Senior Boys 100 Yards
First William Green
I asked him about it,
but before he could reply
Gran said, 'Don't listen to his tales.
The only running he ever did
was after the girls.'
Gramp gave a chuckle
and went out the back
to get the tea.
As he shuffled down the passage
with his back bent,
I tried to imagine him,
legs flying, chest out,
breasting the tape.
But I couldn't.

■ *Readings and Responses*

1   Why can't the poet imagine his grandfather as an athlete?

2   The grandmother and grandfather have a good sense of humour. Where is this shown?

3   There is a very strong contrast in the last six lines. What is being contrasted with what? Refer to specific words in the poem in your answer.

4   Does the family created in this poem seem a happy family? Give your reasons.

5   Many poems deal with the passage of time. Why do you think this is?

To Lauren Newly Born

(also for Jan and Eddie)

Richard Kell

Lauren, your name is lovely —
that *l* and *r* and *n*
a chime melting on water,
easing the hearts of men.

It comes from distant ages
when leaves were heavenly signs,
And Petrarch made it timeless
in passion-haunted lines.

After the sleepy days,
the suckling and the weaning,
you'll give it year by year
your own rich meaning.

I send you now, for love,
a song as small as you,
wishing you faith and courage
whatever life may do.

■ *Reading and Responses*

1 The poet says that his daughter's name, Lauren, is lovely. Write down what you think are the four nicest names (boys' and girls').

2 The poet wishes that his daughter will have faith and courage. What two characteristics would you wish for a young child to have in future years.

3 The poet, Petrarch, mentioned in the second verse, wrote many poems to his loved one, Laura. Do you think this influenced the poet in choosing a name for his daughter?

4 The poet says that the name 'Lauren' is like a 'chime melting on water'. Choose some names and try to say what they suggest to you. You can choose both boys' and girls' names.

5 Some people hate their names so much that they change them by deed poll. Pop stars and film stars often choose new names for themselves. Why are names so important? What do you think of nicknames?

Power Cut

Rita Ann Higgins

Black-out excitement, enchanting,
chasing shadows up and down.

Delirious children play scary
monsters, the walls laugh back.

Father Bear sleeps it off,
dreams of good westerns.

Mother Bear thinks it cultural,
collects young, reads by candle shade.

Siblings content, maternal wing snug,
drifting softly, land of milk and honey.

Father Bear slept enough, weary of culture,
"Try the lights upstairs," he shouts.

Mother Bear switches on. Another culture
shock,
westerns, yoghurt and the late news.

■ *Language and Concepts*

Nuance
Every word has different shades of meaning. These different
shades of meaning are called the nuances of a word. Look at the
different nuances suggested by the following:

    (a) man, bloke, gentleman, guy
    (b) girl, lady, woman, matron.

■ *Readings and Responses*

1 Describe the different reactions of the children, the father and
the mother to the power cut.

2 What kind of atmosphere is suggested by using the terms
Father Bear and Mother Bear?

3 What nuance of meaning is conveyed by the words 'land of
milk and honey'?

4 When the lights came on again, three items are mentioned to
represent the modern world. What three items would you
choose?

Watching My Father Shaving

Basil Payne

Basil Payne said about this poem: 'It is popular with children and adults. I have read it in schools, universities and cultural centres...In all these places the audience laughed (with fear?) during the second half. To me, it is a tragic poem — despite its comic absurdity'.

Watching my father shaving in the kitchen
Before a cracked mirror: This was my four-years-old high-light
In our otherwise humdrum daily domestic ritual.

Mother sliced onions, grey eyes smarting with tears.
Or, scarlet-faced, black-leaded the kitchen range;
Polished the steel parts with fine-grained emery-paper.

Later, she'd do the wash in a zinc bathtub;
Stiffen father's half-dozen shirt collars with Robin Starch
— Father was dapper: starched collar, bow-tie, trim moustache.

Watching him shaving made my intestines tighten;
My eye-balls harden with awe; my heart beats quicken;
That evil steel cut-throat razor — supposing it slipped

On Dad's Adam's apple. Sliced it off. Plop. Like that.
What would I do? Run out to the clothes-line for mother?
Pick it up from the floor; stick it back on his bleeding throat?

It never happened of course: silent, as ordered,
I'd watch him scrape creamy lather from his cheeks,
Chin, neck — such expertise! — then finally throat.

A daily miracle. "There now" (the razor snapped shut),
"I'm sure your mother could do with your help outside."
— Between us, once more, we'd outsmarted honed-up tragedy.

Father died having breakfast (*from natural causes*
The Coroner's verdict recorded). My electric razor purrs.
My young son complains it causes T.V. interference.

■ *Readings and Responses*

1   Do a mime of the father shaving.

2   Why was the child fascinated and frightened by his father shaving?

3   Why are there so many short, sharp phrases in verse five?

4 Why does the author call this a tragic poem? Look particularly at the last verse.

5 Pick out the two most interesting words or phrases in the poem.

The Inter

for Alice Mary

Michael D. Higgins

Watching you preparing for the Inter,
My daughter,
I see in the chaos of your room
A bird
Scratching its nest into shape
And, through your door,
As between branches broken
With violence,
Come my words
That startle.

What value
My distraction
From your task?
Yours was the work of shaping,
Making your own order
In the chaos of others' demands.

Oh, I would that I had come
With a whisper,
Edged one twig towards where you saw it.
But I am burdened with
A catalogue
Of prefabricated designs,
Ugly, efficient and guaranteed
To do the job.

When I come again
I will bring silence,
But know
Even in its noise,
It was love that informed
My bad choice.

Move your twigs
Into the pattern that suits
Your moment
And, not from a distance
I hope
I will look and wonder
At whatever shape
Upon which my love
Rests.

■ *Readings and Responses*

1   The poet's daughter is preparing for her examination in her own way. To what does the poet compare her preparation?

2   The poet offers advice to his daughter but he does this in an awkward way. What words and phrases show this?

3   The poet wanted his daughter to follow his rigid methods. What words show the rigidity of his methods?

4   Family life can be stifling but the poet comes to accept his daughter's individuality. Which lines show this?

5   Describe a teenager's room and say how it reflects his/her personality.

TIMES OF THE YEAR

■

In Ireland we are very interested in the weather because our climate gives us such a variety of weathers. The first comment most people make when they meet is often about the weather. The climate affects the landscape which changes from season to season — from the burnished leaves of autumn to the snows of winter; from the buds of spring to the parched ground of summer.

Last Week in October

December

Xmas

Winter

I Wouldn't Thank You for a Valentine

Spring

■

Last Week in October

Thomas Hardy

The trees are undressing, and fling in many places
On the gray road, the roof, the window-sill —
Their radiant robes and ribbons and yellow laces;
A leaf each second so is flung at will,
Here, there, another and another, still and still.

A spider's web has caught one while downcoming,
That stays there dangling when the rest pass on:
Like a suspended criminal hangs he, mumming,
In golden garb, while one yet green, high yon,
Trembles as fearing such a fate for himself anon.

■ *Language and Concepts*

Extended metaphor
A metaphor is a comparison without the use of the words 'like' or
'as' (see page 15). An extended metaphor is when this comparison
is carried on over a number of lines. For example, in Last Week in
October this metaphor is carried on for five lines.

■ *Readings and Responses*

1   What comparison is made in the first five lines? Trace the
    metaphor through the five lines.

2   There are two very precise, very accurate descriptions in verse
    two. What are they?

3   What is meant by the words 'Like a suspended criminal hangs
    he'?

4   It is said that the eskimos have two hundred words for snow
    and that the desert arabs have a great many words for sand.
    We in Ireland have many words for the different varieties of
    rain. See if you can write at least five words describing the
    different kinds of rain.

5   Write a precise description of today's weather. Avoid clichés
    (see page 94).

December

R. Southey

A wrinkled crabbed man they picture thee,
Old Winter, with a rugged beard as grey
As the long moss upon the apple-tree;
Blue-lipt, an ice drop at thy sharp blue nose,
Close muffled up, and on thy dreary way
Plodding along through sleet and drifting snows.
They should have drawn thee by thy high-heap't hearth
Old Winter! seated in thy great armed chair;
Watching the children at their Christmas mirth; —
Or circled by them as thy lips declare
Some merry jest, or tale of murder dire,
Or troubled spirit that disturbs the night;
Pausing at times to rouse the smouldering fire,
Or taste the old October brown and bright.

■ *Language and Concepts*

Personification
When non-living things are given human characteristics this is
called personification. For example, if 'night' which is non-living,
were personified 'night' could speak and have human feelings. In
the poem above, Winter is regarded as an old man with a beard.
When an idea is personified — treated as if it were living — we
can picture that idea more vividly in our mind.

■ *Readings and Responses*

1   'Winter' is personified in this poem as an old man. What kind
    of old man is 'Winter' in the first six lines?

2   In the last eight lines 'Winter' is still seen as an old man but a
    different kind of old man. What kind of old man is it now seen
    as?

3   Pick out the lines which create the best visual image (picture)
    in your mind.

4   What do you think the 'October brown and bright' is?

5   If you were to personify the following what living thing would
    you make them into: Spring (e.g. Spring is a young lamb
    leaping into the air), Autumn, Death, School, Night, The
    Wind?

Xmas

Wes Magee

Not a twig stirs. The frost-bitten garden
Huddles under a heaped duvet of snow.
Pond, tree, sky and street are granite with cold.

In the house, electronic games warble:
Holly awaits the advent of balloons,
And the TV set glows tipsy with joy.

■ *Language and Concepts*

Clichés
Clichés are old outworn words or phrases which have been used
so many times that they no longer bring any picture to the mind.
Good writers avoid clichés.

■ *Readings and Responses*

1   This poem is called Xmas. What are the different connotations
(see page 80) of the words 'Xmas' and 'Christmas'?

2   The poet just managed to avoid a cliché in line two. Why is
'duvet' a much more vivid word than the cliché he might have
used?

3   There is a powerful contrast between the picture in the first
verse and that in the second verse. Say what this contrast is.

4   Look at the word 'warble'. Can you suggest some words the
poet could have used instead of 'warble' which wouldn't have
been as vivid?

5   'And the TV set glows tipsy with joy.' Describe the scene
suggested by these words.

6   'Christmas has lost its meaning.' Prepare a talk or write an
essay.

Winter

William Shakespeare

When icicles hang by the wall,
    And Dick the shepherd blows his nail,
And Tom bears logs into the hall,
    And milk comes frozen home in pail,
When blood is nipp'd, and ways be foul,
Then nightly sings the staring owl,
            To-whit!
To-who! — a merry note,
While greasy Joan doth keel the pot.

When all aloud the wind doth blow,
    And coughing drowns the parson's saw,
And birds sit brooding in the snow,
    And Marian's nose looks red and raw,
When roasted crabs hiss in the bowl,
Then nightly sings the staring owl,
            To-whit!
To-who! — a merry note,
While greasy Joan doth keel the pot.

■ *Language and Concepts*

Rhyme

Rhyme is to do with words having similar sounds. Two lines of poetry rhyme when the sound of the final syllable at the end of the lines is the same. The way this is notated (or written) is as follows: each rhyme is given a letter of the alphabet, e.g. the first words which rhyme are given the letter 'a', the second set of words which rhyme are given the letter 'b' and so on.

When icicles hang by the wall,	a
And Dick the shepherd blows his nail,	b
And Tom bears logs into the hall,	a
And milk comes frozen home in pail,	b
When blood is nipp'd and ways be foul,	c
Then nightly sings the staring owl,	c

Rhyme helps to make a poem musical but it is only one of the features of the sound of a poem, e.g. alliteration, assonance and rhythm also contribute to the sound of a poem. Not all poems rhyme and rhyme is not essential for a poem to be effective.

1   In this song, Shakespeare gives a lot of details in order to build up a picture of Winter. Which detail conveys the sense of Winter most vividly? Give your reasons.

2   Line fourteen and the last line of each verse present a contrast to all the other details. What is the contrast?

3   All the senses are appealed to in this poem. Find the lines which appeal to the various senses.

4   Try to add some further details of your own which would build up a picture of Winter for you.

5   Notate the rhymes of the whole poem.

I Wouldn't Thank You for a Valentine ('Rap')

Liz Lochhead

I wouldn't thank you for a Valentine.
I won't wake up early wondering if the postman's been.
Should 10 red-padded satin hearts arrive with sticky sickly
    saccharine
Sentiments in very vulgar verses I wouldn't wonder if you meant
    them.
Two dozen anonymous Interflora roses?
I'd not bother to swither over who sent them!
I wouldn't thank you for a Valentine.

Scrawl SWALK across the envelope
I'd just say 'Same Auld Story
I canny be bothered deciphering it -
I'm up to here with Amore!
The whole Valentine's Day Thing is trivial and commercial.
A cue for unleasing cliches and candyheart motifs to which I
    personally am not partial.'
Take more than singing Telegrams, or pints of Chanel Five, or
    sweets,
To get me ordering oysters or ironing my black satin sheets.
I wouldn't thank you for a Valentine.

If you sent me a solitaire and promises solemn.
Took out an ad in the Guardian Personal Column
Saying something very soppy such as 'Who Loves Ya, Poo?
I'll tell you, I do, Fozzy Bear, that's who!'
You'd entirely fail to charm me, in fact I'd detest it
I wouldn't be eighteen again for anything, I'm glad I'm past it.
I wouldn't thank you for a Valentine.

If you sent me a single orchid, or a pair of Janet Reger's in a
    heartshaped box and declared your Love Eternal
I'd say I'd not be caught dead in them they were politically
    suspect and I'd rather something thermal.
If you hired a plane and blazed our love in a banner across the
    skies;
If you bought me something flimsy in a flatteringly wrong size;
If you sent me a postcard with three Xs and told me how you felt
I wouldn't thank you, I'd melt.

■ *Language and Concepts*

'Rap'
'Rap' is a form of poetry which is meant to be recited to a
background of music. It has its origins in urban black America
but has now spread throughout much of the world. 'Rap' allowed
young black people to express their feelings and ideas in their
own way, using slang, local dialect words, 'in' words and coded
language known only to street-smart people.

■ *Readings and Responses*

1   Were you very surprised by the last two words?

2   What is the difference between the postcard mentioned in the
    second last line and all the other Valentines mentioned in the
    rest of the poem?

3   Prepare a performance of this poem. You will need to divide
    into groups. Perhaps two people could deliver the lines
    alternately but the last two lines could be said by the whole
    group. Any performance method which makes the rap vivid is
    acceptable.

4   Find the words to some rap songs. Read them out to the
    class.

5   Do you think St Valentine's Day is trivial and commercial or
    is it just an opportunity for harmless fun? Prepare a talk or
    write an essay.

Spring

Gerard Manley Hopkins

Nothing is so beautiful as spring —
   When weeds, in wheels, shoot long and lovely and lush;
   Thrush's eggs look little low heavens, and thrush
Through the echoing timber does so rinse and wring
The ear, it strikes like lightnings to hear him sing;
   The glassy peartree leaves and blooms, they brush
   The descending blue; that blue is all in a rush
With richness; the racing lambs too have fair their fling.
What is all this juice and all this joy?
   A strain of the earth's sweet being in the beginning
In Eden garden. — Have, get, before it cloy,
   Before it cloud, Christ, Lord, and sour with sinning,
Innocent mind and Mayday in girl and boy,
   Most, O maid's child, thy choice and worthy the winning.

■ *Language and Concepts*

Poetic licence
Poets sometimes take liberties with the strict rules of grammar which govern how we ordinarily write. They do this not because they don't know the rules, but because they wish to create their effects more vividly. In *Spring* Hopkins leaves out words and changes the normal order of words and clauses. These changes arouse our attention and make us see things anew. Hopkins wants us to experience the newness and the freshness of Spring so he uses language which is as new and as fresh as he can make it. He wants to 'shock' us into attention.

■ *Readings and Responses*

1   This poem is a sonnet (see page 20). What idea is presented in the octave? What development is presented in the sestet?

2   Can you find where there is the appeal to the various senses? Look at words such as 'cloy', 'rinse' 'sour', etc. ˙

3   There are many examples of alliteration. Pick out three.

4   This is a poem about the wonder and beauty of Spring but it is also about innocence. Explain. It might help to know Gerard Manley Hopkins was a Jesuit priest.

5   Write your own description of Spring..

MICHEÁL Ó SIADHAIL

■

Mícheál Ó Siadhail is married and lives in Dublin. He attended Clongowes Wood College, Co. Kildare. He has worked as a University lecturer, but he is now a full-time writer.

Easter

Espousal

Visit

Initiation

Schoolboy Final

Fashion Show

■

Easter

Mícheál Ó Siadhail

Dizzy with joy, the Easter morning
Sun trembles in the heavens;
The tacky buds unclenched, release
An appropriate festschrift of leaves.

Unsuspected, in their microworld
Infinitesimal cells teem, crossplay,
Rich networks of twisted strings
Interlace, relate to the concord

Of history rebegun. A starling mimics
Bravura, woodpigeons whoop it up,
The orchestra purrs, tunes into
A master craftsman. Life *da capo*,

As riding our whirling earth-ship
We zip around the sun;
Umpteen billion miles apart
Stars both giant and dwarf

Are suns that tug their planets,
Constellate, take their partners,
Dance the zillionhanded reel,
Pinwheel outwards to eternity.

Glimpsing an infinitude of perfection,
Awestruck, half-enlightened man
Refracts the marvel, magnifies
The all-inclusive Easter thought.

■ *Readings and Responses*

1 Easter is the great festival of Spring and the rebirth of nature.
   How is this suggested in the first verse?

2 What is the poet attempting to describe in the second verse?

3 What orchestra is the poet referring to in verse three? Who are
   the players? Who is the composer, the 'master craftsman'?

4 The poet spoke of the 'microworld' in verse two. In contrast,
   what does he refer to in verses four and five?

5 What does the poet say about man in the last verse? What is
   man's reaction to the wonders of Spring? Is there a religious
   nuance in the last line?

The following three poems are about Ó Siadhail's first few months in Clongowes Wood College as a boarder. Ó Siadhail says about boarding school: 'I begged to go to boarding school ... there was bullying — I was big and tall and well able to look after myself ... I wouldn't paint it black and white. The plus side of it was that I came to value friendship all my life ... the overall feeling is that it's sad to lose the kitchen in the evening and the balance of male and female company, though I recognise that there are circumstances where it might be necessary and sometimes — say, there is an overpowering parent — where a person might even blossom.'

(Interview in *The Irish Times*, 13/1/91)

Espousal

Mícheál Ó Siadhail

Days early my trousseau lay in the hallway,
Mother's own school trunk newly hinged,
freighted as prescribed — all regalia
taped and numbered: rug, napkin ring,
tuck box, laundry bags. Hour by hour
a dreamy September holds its breath.

Late evening, a scuffle of gravel as cars
brake on the castle's forecourt. Novices
reconnoitre, bustle of arrivals, goodbyes,
last advices and already I fidget, eager
to embrace my venture; parting promises:
a visit in a fortnight; waves in the half-light.

Down the marble steps into the vast
corridor of wainscotting and notice boards,
lists of placings for study-hall and chapel;
chance meetings, the territory explored —
playrooms, libraries. The tug of a bell,
a hush and we file towards night prayers.

So, this is the honeymoon of my fantasy,
a reverie of quads, pillow fights, decent
chaps with parcels and cads in Coventry....
My friend was coming, I begged to be sent.
'You're on your own', father has warned,
'you've made your bed, now lie in it'.

Ten twenty. Lights out in the Holy Angels,
we slide into iron beds; a skittish
silence falls; in earshot another dormitory,
same prayer, commanding flick of switch.
Neighbours whisper introductions: Michael
Walls, Roscommon; Flannery from Tipperary.

Snatches of a parlance, subliminal spells:
all out, lectio brevis, night-squares,
smoke in the mind; days to come
gleam, a jingling clump of mortise keys.
I espouse a new world, drop into sleep;
expectation whirrs in the tongues of bells.

■ *Language and Concepts*

Jargon/Parlance

Jargon is the particular language which has to do with some job, place, game, activity. Jargon can sometimes involve technical terms which can only be understood by initiates, that is, those who are involved in the activity concerned. Jargon is often criticised as 'gobbledygook', that is, nonsense. Jargon is not gobbledygook if it is used to those who know the vocabulary. Therefore, jargon is like slang: it is alright in its own place but should not be used if the hearer is unlikely to understand it.

Parlance means more or less the same as jargon except that parlance is not criticised as often as jargon is.

■ *Readings and Responses*

1   A sense of expectation is created in the first verse. What lines particularly evoke this feeling?

2   What scene is created in the second verse?

3   What is meant by 'you've made your bed, now lie in it'?

    From where had the poet obtained his idea of what a boarding school would be like? Look at the first three lines of verse four.

4   What mood is evoked by: 'days to come/gleam' and by 'expectation whirrs in the tongues of bells.'?

5   'Snatches of a parlance'. 'Parlance' means words associated with some job, place or activity. Is there a particular 'school parlance' and a particular 'games parlance'? Give examples.

Visit

Mícheál Ó Siadhail

Sunday afternoon about three o'clock
('with prior permission from your prefect')
pewed in a car on the gravel forecourt
our talk swivels between two worlds.
Angling herself in the passenger seat
my mother turns her face to me;
awkward behind a steering wheel, father's
eye catches mine in his rear-view mirror.

I rehearse this scene trying to read
my mother's face wondering if she sensed
I had left for good — son and emigré.
Four months' days ticked off a calendar,
at last I'd return, a displaced guest,
uneasy with neighbours, missing school friends,
my eye proportioned to halls and arches
and home diminished as a doll's house.

Family doings, bulletins from a neighbourhood,
mention of names, small emissaries
of emotion from suburban roads, old
gravities draw me for a moment homeward.
And I resist. We are visitors for each other.
Unwittingly those weeks of initiation leave
a baffle between us. Our words fall short.
I am learning a new language, another lore.

■ *Readings and Responses*

1   Describe the scene in the car.

2   What is meant by: 'our talk swivels between two worlds.'?

3   Explain the lines:

'my eye proportioned to halls and arches
and home diminished as a doll's house.'

4   'I am learning a new language.' Does the poet just mean the
school 'parlance' or is he referring to something else?

5   Have you ever been away from home for a time — at school,
on holiday, in hospital? When you came home did home
appear different? Write about this experience.

Initiation

Mícheál Ó Siadhail

By hearsay beginners fear the passage rite:
dark talk of toilet dousing and shamings.
Watch your step. Last year's weaklings lord
a brief revenge — *old scout's preference*.
To endure is everything, so now bide time.
Day by day the hierarchical bluff is called.
Seats at table fixed by scramble, the head
holds sway, portions out the food at whim,
waylaying second helpings for his table-top
cronies. It's Monday. Roly-poly and custard
for dessert; O'Sullivan acts the tough, threatens
to confiscate my share.... Outside I tackle him;
a flurry of punches, I fall in a stranglehold.
Days later another flare-up; again he wins.
His taboo endangered, we have settled down
to a sultry peace. Fantasy slips into reality.
Inmates of a world slowly, slowly enamoured
of our narrow purlieus, every rule and loophole,
bounds and out of bounds, little by little
we grow fond of our containment. After dinner
in the hamper-room cutting a slice of cake
one of *the hards* comes wheedling, menacing
give us a scrounge! Swear at him loudly —
grinning, he moves on. The weeks pass,
the fittest thrive. No Joyce, no Stephen Dedalus,
your ghost may sulk on the Third Line crease,
baulk at our scramble, but your gaze is hindsight.
We think we dream of home and all the while
who got *sleeps* or a parcel, who made the team,
shifts of comradeship, rumours of a prefect's mood,
concerns, subterfuges map our hours and fill
an atlas of our living. We're in love with survival.
All other worlds are slipping out of reach.

■ *Readings and Responses*

1 What is meant by 'initiation' and 'passage rite'? Can you think
of other areas of life where there are initiation rites?

2 'Fantasy slips into reality.' What does the poet mean by this?
Look at the fourth verse of *Espousal* for a clue about the fantasy.

3 Pick out words from school parlance used in this poem.

4 What is meant by 'We're in love with survival./ All other
worlds are slipping out of reach.'?

5 What impression of boarding school life is given to you by this
poem?

Schoolboy final

Mícheál Ó Siadhail

At each corner flagsellers double deal.
Colour-parties of schoolboys stump, file
Through the turnstiles, bustling on to the stands.

The hub-bub swells while banners, mascots
Swirl and vie: already togged cheerleaders
Megaphone their slogans. One commissar

Glancing towards the field eyes someone's
Sister among the schoolgirl campfollowers;
Concentration wavers, resumes as a battlecry.

Huddled between factions, inwardly fluttering
Parents affect a sangfroid 'Yes let's hope
they are evenly matched.' A warrior-priest chainsmokes.

Furore. Two squads erupt into the arena,
Flexing, limbering. A pent-up frenzy
Steadies, runs up, kicks. Life is in parenthesis.

The sun raids the pitch, angling spring-light
Past the grandstand gable; the crowds chant
Surges and slumps as chance twirls the volume.

A loose ruck, the ball tunnelled back, picked
Up, a long looping pass, well-gathered, chipped
Forward. On the attack. Commenting in the lingo

The old timers' adrenalin empathises; reruns,
Trailers, inklings of cosmos within cosmos reconnoitre
Life as an enthusiasm. The world turns seventeen.

■ *Language and Concepts*

Sporting clichés

Clichés are old, outworn words or phrases. Sports writing is particularly prone to them, e.g. 'over the moon', 'it's a funny old game'. Good writers avoid clichés. Notice how Mícheal Ó Siadhail avoids clichés.

■ *Readings and Responses*

1   What words in the first two verses suggest the sense of excitement and noise on the way to the match?

2   What is the attitude of the adults at the match?

3   Why are there so many short phrases with so many commas in verse seven?

4   Choose a period of ten minutes from a game or sport. You can choose just before or after the game. Write about this ten minutes avoiding clichés.

Fashion Show

Mícheál Ó Siadhail

Out in the daylight green is the rage,
Chlorophyll the mode. Trees let it all
Hang out while indoors poor leafless
Sophisticates of shape and dye present
A spring collection. Quietly sensational
In magenta, lilac, beige or stone
High stepping ladies arm for summer.

Models turn our heads with readymade
Come-hither smiles, lope in their spotlight
Circle, splash their favours of layering
And fabric, whisk past in giddy colours;
A final bout, then swishing down the steps,
Unbuttoning, they breakneck for a cubicle.
We await another creation. Meantime

Three new mannequins swirl on stage,
Ambush the eye; the compere patters on:
'Now a summerdress in china blue
With scalloped hem.' How can they dream
Up such stratagems, the tuck and cut
To self-assure, frazzle the male to ask
No whys or wherefores. O lovely woman!

No! Stop! The tease will unman me —
If only they would speak, say something
Unreasonable to slow desire, but those
Body linguists will show no leniency,
Beaming all the more they swoop
Across the platform. Bewitched again,
Fall a little for these frame-dames!

■ *Readings and Responses*

1   Act out the scene in this poem.

2   In the first verse the poet deliberately mixes up the language
of nature and the language of fashion. Show how he does this.

3   How do the mannequins 'ambush the eye'?

4   What is meant by the phrase 'body linguists'?

5   'You can tell all about a person from their clothes and
hairstyle.' Give three illustrations to prove this statement.

MAKING YOUR MIND UP; OPTIONS FOR LIFE

We are responsible for our own lives and life is full of options and decisions: How long will we stay at school? What job will we do? Who will we marry? What kind of person will we be? To be fully human is to be able to consider the options and make choices.

Alter Ego

The Choosing

The Road not Taken

Dark Memories

Alter Ego

Dennis O'Driscoll

At times, I wish I had been able
to stay on in the home place
rounding up a few cows with the dog
having decided to give America a skip.

On Sundays, I'd take up a stick
and follow the reedy river in my suit
or lean over after Mass
to hear the chat of neighbours,
inclining toward each other
like old blotchy gravestones.

There would be a corner of hay to save,
a stack of firewood to cut and dry,
a parish club to cheer when evenings stretched,
ballads to tap a foot to in the pub.

It would be nice to see a friendly face
an odd time at the window;
a few letters — but no handwriting I'd dread.
I might have been one of those
dark characters in caps, saluting everyone,
who cycle stealthily into the town,
fixing you with a robin's scrutinising eye.

I'd keep the cottage door open from June onwards
to let in summer smells, sounds of peaty streams;
hedges blossoming with small bells;
thin-sliced wing-wrapped butterflies
alighting on my buddleia bush.

With no one's welfare but my own to care for,
I'd accept age and death with resignation.
I could have been happy that way, maybe,
walking the spotless fields on frosty mornings
or snug in knitted socks beside the grate.
On winter nights, my outside light
would perforate the dark.

■ *Language and Concepts*

Nostalgia
Nostalgia is a yearning for past times. Some elderly people and some emigrants experience strong feelings of nostalgia for the past.

1   What kind of life do you think the speaker in this poem has?

2   Does he have a realistic view of country life or is he too nostalgic? Does he refer anywhere to the harsher aspects of country life?

3   What decision did the speaker in this poem take at some time in his life?

4   What is the most pleasant scene painted by the speaker of the life he might have led?

5   Do you think he would have been contented if he had stayed at home?

The Choosing

Liz Lochhead

We were first equal Mary and I
with the same coloured ribbons in mouse-coloured hair,
and with equal shyness
we curtseyed to the Lady councillor
for copies of Collins' Children's Classics.
First equal, equally proud.

Best friends too Mary and I
a common bond in being cleverest (equal)
in our small school's small class.
I remember
the competition for top desk
or to read aloud the lesson
at school service.
And my terrible fear
of her superiority at sums.

I remember the housing scheme
Where we both stayed.
The same house, different homes,
where the choices were made.

I don't know exactly why they moved,
but anyway they went.

Something about a three-apartment
and a cheaper rent.
But from the top deck of the high-school bus
I'd glimpse among the others on the corner
Mary's father, mufflered, contrasting strangely
with the elegant greyhounds by his side.
He didn't believe in high-school education,
especially for girls,
or in forking out for uniforms.

Ten years later on a Saturday —
I am coming home from the library —
sitting near me on the bus,
Mary
with a husband who is tall,
curly haired, has eyes
for no one else but Mary.
Her arms are round the full-shaped vase
that is her body.
Oh, you can see where the attraction lies
in Mary's life —
not that I envy her, really.

And I am coming from the library
with my arms full of books.
I think of the prizes that were ours for the taking
and wonder when the choices got made
we don't remember making.

■ *Readings and Responses*

1 Describe the two different lifestyles of the girls now.

2 What is the relationship between Mary and her husband?
   Pick out the words which show this relationship.

3 Is Mary content with her life? Comment on the phrase 'the
   full-shaped vase'.

4 Does the author envy Mary?

5 What is the meaning of the last two lines?

The Road not Taken

Robert Frost

Two roads diverged in a yellow wood,
And sorry I could not travel both
And be one traveller, long I stood
And looked down one as far as I could
To where it bent in the undergrowth;

Then took the other, as just as fair,
And having perhaps the better claim,
Because it was grassy and wanted wear;
Though as for that the passing there
Had worn them really about the same,

And both that morning equally lay
In leaves no step had trodden black.
Oh, I kept the first for another day!
Yet knowing how way leads on to way,
I doubted if I should ever come back.

I shall be telling this with a sigh
Somewhere ages and ages hence:
Two roads diverged in a wood, and I –
I took the one less travelled by,
And that has made all the difference.

■ *Language and Concepts*

Theme
The theme of a poem is the main idea contained in the poem. You should be able to state the approximate theme of a poem in one or two sentences.

■ *Readings and Responses*

1   What reason does the poet give for choosing one road other than the other?

2   What is the theme of this poem?

3   Is the road meant to be just a road or is it a symbol for something else?

4   What kind of life do you think the person in this poem eventually led?

5   What do you think is the most important decision you will have to make over the next few years? How can a person prepare so that they can make the right decision?

Dark Memories

Michael D. Higgins

Sitting in a dark room, she'd ask me
Not to turn on the light,
That her tears might not be seen.
We'd know it was like that
For, earlier she might have said,
If I was starting out again,
It's into a convent I'd have gone,
Away from all the trouble.
Or she would have spoken
Of lovely times in the shop, drinking
Tea and eating Marietta biscuits,
Or taking a walk with her little dog,
After playing the piano in the sitting-room
Over the shop, where soldiers came
And bought more biscuits, when life
Was easy in Liscarroll,
A garrison town; before my father
Blew up railway lines and courted his way
Into her affections.

She stood straight then, and, in a long leather coat,
After her mother died she packed her case
Left and joined him a full decade after
The Civil War. And she had loved him
In her way. Even when Old Binchy placed a note
Behind the counter in his shop
In Charleville that when all this blackguardism
Was over, there would be no jobs
For Republicans in his firm, or anywhere else,
For that matter.

Now bent and leaning towards the fire,
With blackened fingers holding the tongs,
She poked the coals; and we knew,
It best to leave her with her sorrow
For her lost life, the house she'd lost,
The anxious days and nights,
And all that might have been.

We ran outside and brought in turf
And did our lessons and vowed that we would listen
To what she said, of cities where always
There were voices for company, and churches
Close by, if never cheap.
We would listen to her story
And vow that, for her at least
We, her children, would escape.

■ *Readings and Responses*

1   In this poem the mother sometimes feels that if she had her
    life over again she would have made different choices. Why
    might she have made a different choice?

2   Describe some of the happy memories she has.

3   How is it shown in the third section that she was a woman of
    determined character?

4   Why do the children vow to escape?

5   Why does the mother feel that her life was a 'lost life'?

JOHN MONTAGUE

■

John Montague was born in Brooklyn, New York in 1929. He lived for a time in France. He was a lecturer in University College, Cork for many years. He has also published short stories.

The Trout

The Cage

The Silver Flask

Windharp

The Country Fiddler

■

The Trout

John Montague

Flat on the bank I parted
Rushes to ease my hands
In the water without a ripple
And tilt them slowly downstream
To where he lay, tendril light,
In his fluid sensual dream.

Bodiless lord of creation
I hung briefly above him
Savouring my own absence
Senses expanding in the slow
Motion, the photographic calm
That grows before action.

As the curve of my hands
Swung under his body
He surged, with visible pleasure.
I was so preternaturally close
I could count every stipple
But still cast no shadow, until

The two palms crossed in a cage
Under the lightly pulsing gills.
Then (entering my own enlarged
Shape, which rode on the water)
I gripped. To this day I can
Taste his terror on my hands.

■ *Language and Concepts*

Climax/Anti-climax
The climax of a poem or story is the point of highest excitement when the build-up of tension is dissolved.
An anti-climax occurs when there is the build-up of tension to an expected high point of excitement but then no event takes place to resolve the problem.

■ Readings and Responses

1 Describe what happens in this poem.
2 What is conveyed by the words 'tendril light'?
3 What is meant by 'the photographic calm/That grows before action'?
4 How is the tension built up? Where does the climax occur? Pick out the one word which is climactic.

The Cage

John Montague

My father, the least happy
man I have known. His face
retained the pallor
of those who work underground:
the lost years in Brooklyn
listening to a subway
shudder the earth.

But a traditional Irishman
who (released from his grille
in the Clark St I.R.T.)
drank neat whiskey until
he reached the only element
he felt at home in
any longer: brute oblivion.

And yet picked himself
up, most mornings,
to march down the street
extending his smile
to all sides of the good
(non-negro) neighbourhood
belled by St Teresa's church.

When he came back
we walked together
across fields of Garvaghey
to see hawthorn on the summer
hedges, as though
he had never left;
a bend of the road

which still sheltered
primroses. But we
did not smile in
the shared complicity
of a dream, for when
weary Odysseus returns
Telemachus must leave.

Often as I descend
into subway or underground
I see his bald head behind

the bars of the small booth;
the mark of an old car
accident beating on his
ghostly forehead.

■ *Readings and Responses*

1   What kind of life did the poet's father lead in New York?

2   Why is the poem called *The Cage?*

3   Did the poet's father ever really settle in New York? Look particularly at the fourth verse.

4   How would you describe the mood of the last verse? Give reasons for your answer.

5   'Emigration — always a tragedy.' Prepare a talk or write an essay.

The Silver Flask

John Montague

Sweet, though short, our
hours as a family together.
Driving across dark mountains
to Midnight Mass in Fivemiletown,
lights coming up in the valleys
as in the days of Carleton.

Tussocks of heather brown
in the headlights; our mother
stowed in the back, a tartan
rug wrapped round her knees,
patiently listening as father sang
and the silver flask went round.

Chorus after chorus of the *Adoremus*
to shorten the road before us,
till *we see amidst the winter's snows*
the festive lights of the small town
and from the choirloft an organ booms
angels we have heard on high, with

my father joining warmly in,
his broken tenor soaring, faltering,
a legend in dim bars of Brooklyn
(that sacramental moment of stillness
among exiled, disgruntled men)
now raised vehemently once again

in the valleys he had sprung from,
startling the stiff congregation
with fierce blasts of song, while
our mother sat silent beside him,
sad but proud, an unaccustomed
blush mantling her wan countenance.

Then driving slowly home,
tongues crossed with the communion
wafer, snowflakes melting in
the car's hungry headlights,
till we reach the warm kitchen
and the spirits round again.

The family circle briefly restored
nearly twenty lonely years after
that last Christmas in Brooklyn,
under the same tinsel of decorations
so carefully hoarded by our mother
in the cabin trunk of a Cunard liner.

■ *Language and Concepts*

The setting of a poem
There are three different scenes in *The Silver Flask*, thus the
poem has three different settings or places where the action
happens.

■ *Readings and Responses*

1   What are the three different settings of the action of this
    poem?

2   Look at verse five. Why do you think the mother began to
    blush?

3   There is a rich appeal to four of our five senses in this poem.
    Trace this appeal through the poem.

4   What do you think is the most vivid image in this poem? Try
    to put the image in your own words.

5   Try to describe a Midnight Mass or other religious service of
    your experience in as interesting a way as John Montague
    has done.

Windharp

for Patrick Collins

John Montague

The sounds of Ireland,
that restless whispering
you never get away
from, seeping out of
low bushes and grass,
heatherbells and fern,
wrinkling bog pools,
scraping tree branches,
light hunting cloud,
sound hounding sight,
a hand ceaselessly
combing and stroking
the landscape, till
the valley gleams
like the pile upon
a mountain pony's coat.

■ *Language and Concepts*

Assonance and Internal Alliteration
Assonance is similar sounding vowel sounds, e.g. the 'ou' sound
in 'sound, hounding' and the 'o' sound in 'combing and stroking'.
There is internal alliteration (similar consonontal sounds) in the
'restless whispering'. It is very appropriate that such musical
effects should be present in this poem which suggests that the
sound of the 'windharp' is somehow present in all things Irish.

■ *Readings and Responses*

1   What is suggested by the words 'seeping out'?

2   This poem seems to suggest that the landscape of Ireland is
    like a vast 'windharp' being played. Show where this is
    suggested.

3   The poet doesn't refer anywhere to towns or cities. Comment
    on this.

4   This poem conveys that sense of longing felt by an emigrant.
    If you left Ireland or if you left your town or area what five
    aspects of life or features of the area would you miss most of
    all?

The Country Fiddler

John Montague

The poet's uncle went to the U.S. The poet was a child living in the U.S. and then came to Ireland. Twenty years later he went back to America.

My uncle played the fiddle — more elegantly the violin —
A favourite at barn and cross-roads dance,
He knew *The Sailor's bonnet* and *The Fowling Piece*.

Bachelor head of a house full of sisters,
Runner of poor racehorses, spendthrift,
He left for the New World in an old disgrace.

He left his fiddle in the rafters
When he sailed, never played afterwards;
A rural art silenced in the discord of Brooklyn.

A heavily-built man, tranquil-eyed as an ox,
He ran a wild speakeasy, and died of it.
During the depression many dossed in his cellar.

I attended his funeral in the Church of the Redemption,
Then, unexpected successor, reversed time
To return where he had been born.

During my schooldays the fiddle rusted
(The bridge fell away, the catgut snapped)
Reduced to a plaything stinking of stale rosin.

The country people asked if I also had music
(all the family had had) but the fiddle was in pieces
And the rafters remade, before I discovered my craft.

Twenty years afterwards, I saw the church again,
And promised to remember my burly godfather
And his rural craft, after this fashion:

So succession passes, through strangest hands.

■ *Readings and Responses*

1   What artistic talent did the uncle have?

2   What kind of man was the uncle? Did his character change when he went to the U.S.? Look at the second and fourth verse.

3   What is meant by 'A rural art silenced in the discord of Brooklyn'?

THE LIVING WORLD

Awareness of the wonder of animals and respect for their dignity is increasingly seen as one mark of civilization. In the following seven poems the world of animals and birds, in all its variety and majesty, is explored.

'We Are Going to See the Rabbit ...'

The Swan

The Donkey

The Tom Cat

Tim

Interruption to a Journey

Travelling Through the Dark

'We Are Going to See the Rabbit...'
Alan Brownjohn

We are going to see the rabbit,
We are going to see the rabbit.
Which rabbit, people say?
Which rabbit, ask the children?
Which rabbit?
The only rabbit,
The only rabbit in England,
Sitting behind a barbed-wire fence
Under the floodlights, neon lights,
Sodium lights,
Nibbling grass
On the only patch of grass
In England, in England
(Except the grass by the hoardings
Which doesn't count.)
We are going to see the rabbit
And we must be there on time.

First we shall go by escalator,
Then we shall go by underground,
And then we shall go by motorway
And then by helicopterway,
And the last ten yards we shall have to go
On foot.

And now we are going
All the way to see the rabbit.
We are nearly there,
We are longing to see it,
And so is the crowd
Which is here in thousands
With mounted policemen
And big loudspeakers
And bands and banners,
And everyone has come a long way.
But soon we shall see it
Sitting and nibbling
The blades of grass
On the only patch of grass
In — but something has gone wrong!
Why is everyone so angry,
Why is everyone jostling
And slanging and complaining?

The rabbit has gone,
Yes, the rabbit has gone.
He has actually burrowed down into the earth
And made himself a warren, under the earth,
Despite all these people.
And what shall we do?
What can we do?

It is all a pity, you must be disappointed,
Go home and do something else for today,
Go home again, go home for today.
For you cannot hear the rabbit, under the earth.
Remarking rather sadly to himself, by himself,
As he rests in his warren, under the earth:
'It won't be long, they are bound to come,
they are bound to come and find me, even here.'

■ *Language and Concepts*

Science fiction
This could be called a science fiction poem. Science fiction deals with the future and suggests what might happen if particular scientific discoveries are made and acted upon. 'Dr Who' and 'Star Trek' are science fiction television programmes.

■ *Readings and Responses*

1   This poem presents a bleak vision of society in the future. What does it suggest might happen?

2   The first section contrasts the artificial and the natural. What represents the artificial and what represents the natural?

3   Even though everybody is coming to see the rabbit, the rabbit itself fears that it will be killed. Does the rest of the poem suggest that its fears might be justified?

4   Everyone is 'angry', 'jostling', 'slanging', 'complaining'. Does this tell us anything about the state of this society?

5   The destruction of the environment: how far will it go in the future? Prepare a talk or write on this subject.

The Swan

Richard Kell

Nothing more serene than the fluid neck,
the body curved like snow on foliage,
and spilt reflection moving smooth as oil.

But something wrecks the tranquil certainty:
the clean-cut shape unfolds; an evil wind
tears its roots out of the fertile water.

The pattern's tugged awry — the neck rammed stiff,
cumbrous wings whacking the startled air —
and terror swirls the surface of the lake.

■ *Readings and Responses*

1   What words are used to describe the gracefulness of the swan?

2   What happens in the second verse?

3   Pick out the words which most vividly describe the gracelessness of the swan in flight.

4   This poem is built upon a contrast. What is the contrast?

5   Describe the most graceful animal/bird you can and then describe the most graceless animal/bird you can.

The Donkey

G.K.Chesterton

When fishes flew and forests walked
   And figs grew upon thorn,
Some moment when the moon was blood
   Then surely I was born.

With monstrous head and sickening cry
   And ears like errant wings,
The devil's walking parody
   On all four-footed things.

The tattered outlaw of the earth,
   Of ancient crooked will,
Starve, scourge, deride me: I am dumb
   I keep my secret still.

Fools! For I also had my hour;
   One far fierce hour and sweet:
There was a shout about my ears,
   And palms before my feet.

■ *Language and Concepts*

Explicit and implicit meaning
When the words openly and directly state their meaning this is explicit language. Sometimes it is better just to suggest or hint at the meaning so as to make the readers create the picture themselves in their own minds. When the meaning is only suggested or hinted at, the meaning is implicit.

■ *Readings and Responses*

1   'A camel is a horse designed by a committee.' The donkey also feels he is a somewhat ridiculous, bizarre-looking creature. Where is this stated in the poem?

2   This poem is divided into two parts. The first part describes the oddness of the donkey. What word signals the beginning of the second part?

3   Is the donkey's moment of glory explicitly stated? Note, for example, that there is no mention of Christ or Jerusalem. Must we supply the full meaning ourselves?

4   What was the donkey's moment of glory?

5   Try to invent four or five imaginary occurrences as impossible as 'when fishes flew and forests walked'.

The Tom Cat

Don Marquis

At midnight in the alley
A Tom Cat comes to wail,
And he chants the hate of a million years
As he swings his snaky tail.

Malevolent, bony, brindled,
Tiger and devil and bard,
His eyes are coals from the middle of Hell
And his heart is black and hard.

He twists and crouches and capers
And bares his curved sharp claws,
And he sings to the stars of the jungle nights,
Ere cities were, or laws.

Beast from a world primeval,
He and his leaping clan,
When the blotched red moon leers over the roofs,
Give voice to their scorn of man.

He will lie on a rug tomorrow
And lick his silky fur,
And veil the brute in his yellow eyes
And play he's tame, and purr.

But at midnight in the alley
He will crouch again and wail,
And beat the time of his demon's song
With the swing of his demon's tail.

■ *Language and Concepts*

Ambiguous words or attitudes

An ambiguous word is a word whose meaning is not clear and is capable of more than one interpretation. If a person's attitude is ambiguous their attitude is capable of more than one interpretation. For example, a person may have an ambiguous attitude to the use of violence. We can't be certain whether they are for it or against it. In the poem *The Tom Cat* the cat seems to have an ambiguous attitude to man.

■ *Readings and Responses*

1   In the first two verses what words allow us to 'see' and 'hear' the Tom Cat?

2   What words in the second and third verses suggest that the
    Tom Cat is very tough and is very capable of looking after
    himself?

3   What picture of the Tom Cat is given in verse five?

4   Has the Tom Cat an ambiguous attitude to man? Look at the
    fourth and fifth verses.

5   Remember a creature you have watched closely. Write four or
    five observations, each one relating to a separate sense (sight,
    touch, hearing, taste, smell).

Tim

John Montague

Not those slim-flanked fillies
slender-ankled as models
glimpsed across the rails
through sunlong afternoons
as with fluent fetlocks
they devoured the miles

Nor at some Spring Show
a concourse of Clydesdales
waiting, huge as mammoths,
as enormous hirsute dolls,
for an incongruous rose to
blossom behind their ears

Nor that legendary Pegasus
leaping towards heaven:
only those hold my affection
who, stolid as weights,
stood in the rushy
meadows of my childhood

Or rumbled down lanes,
lumbering before carts.
Tim, the first horse I rode,
seasick on his barrel
back; the first to lip
bread from my hand.

I saw the end of your road.
You stood, with gouged eyeball
while our farmhand swabbed
the hurt socket out with
water and Jeyes Fluid:
as warm an object of

loving memory as any
who have followed me
to this day, denying
rhetoric with your patience,
forcing me to drink
from the trough of reality.

■ *Language and Concepts*

Rhetoric

A word can sometimes have a number of meanings. 'Rhetoric' is such a word.

(a) A rhetorical question is a question that really doesn't require an answer because the person asking the question already knows the answer. For example, 'Isn't it a lovely day?' is not a question that requires an answer because you already know the answer.

(b) Students in ancient universities studied rhetoric which is the art of speaking or writing effectively. Your present English course is very like this.

(c) The most usual meaning of the word rhetoric today is insincere or exaggerated language. Somebody might say about a politician's speech that it was full of rhetoric, i.e. he or she didn't really mean what they were saying.

■ *Readings and Responses*

1 What kind of horse is presented in verse one?

2 What kind of horse is presented in verse two?

3 There are three similes in the first two verses. What are they? Which of them do you think is the most vivid?

4 Which of the three senses of the word rhetoric is used in the last verse?

5 What is meant by 'forcing me to drink/from the trough of reality'?

Interruption to a Journey

Norman MacCaig

The hare we had run over
Bounced about the road
On the springing curve
Of its spine.

Cornfields breathed in the darkness,
We were going through the darkness and
The breathing cornfields from one
Important place to another.

We broke the hare's neck
And made that place, for a moment,
The most important place there was,
Where a bowstring was cut
And a bow broken forever
That had shot itself through so many
Darknesses and cornfields.

It was left in that landscape
It left us in another.

■ *Readings and Responses*

1   How would you describe the poet's tone of voice when he says
    'one/Important place to another'?

2   The poet then says:
    'And made that place, for a moment,/The most important
    place there was'
    To whom was it the most important place?

3   Were the people in the car changed by the event? Look at the
    last two lines. How were they changed?

4   Pick out lines which show how fragile life is.

5   Have you ever experienced an event similar to that described
    in the poem? Write about it, explaining what the experience
    meant to you.

Travelling Through the Dark
William Stafford

Travelling through the dark I found a deer
dead on the edge of the Wilson River road.
It is usually best to roll them into the canyon:
that road is narrow; to swerve might make more dead.

By glow of the tail-light I stumbled back of the car
and stood by the heap, a doe, a recent killing;
she had stiffened already, almost cold.
I dragged her off; she was large in the belly.

My fingers touching her side brought me the reason —
her side was warm; her fawn lay there waiting,
alive, still, never to be born.
Beside that mountain road I hesitated.

The car aimed ahead its lowered parking lights;
under the hood purred the steady engine.
I stood in the glare of the warm exhaust turning red;
around our group I could hear the wilderness listen.

I thought hard for us all — my only swerving —
then pushed her over the edge into the river.

■ *Language and Concepts*

Evocative language
Evocative words are words that powerfully evoke or bring to mind
what the writer wishes to describe. A good writer will use
evocative language that will vividly convey his/her meaning.

■ *Readings and Responses*

1   The doe had already stiffened but her side was warm. Why?

2   Do you feel that the poet has a reverence for life? Can he do
anything about it?

3   There is perhaps a contrast suggested between the
mechanical and the living. What is this contrast?

4   What is meant by 'I could hear the wilderness listen'?

5   Read *Interruption to a Journey* (page 130). What are the
similarities between the two poems? Which poem uses the
more evocative language?

PATRICK KAVANAGH

Patrick Kavanagh was born in 1906 on a small farm in Inniskeen, Co. Monaghan. He received no formal post-primary education. He worked on the farm until he moved to Dublin in 1939. He wrote the novel *Tarry Flynn* and an autobiographical work *The Green Fool*. Kavanagh's poetry has influenced many of the younger generation of Irish poets.

from Tarry Flynn

In Memory of My Mother

A Christmas Childhood

Spraying the Potatoes

from Tarry Flynn

Patrick Kavanagh

On an apple-ripe September morning
through the mist-chill fields I went
With a pitch-fork on my shoulder
Less for use than for devilment.

The threshing mill was set-up, I knew,
In Cassidy's haggard last night,
And we owed them a day at the threshing
Since last year. O it was delight

To be paying bills of laughter
And chaffy gossip in kind
With work thrown in to ballast
The fantasy-soaring mind.

As I crossed the wooden bridge I wondered
As I looked into the drain
If ever a summer morning should find me
Shovelling up eels again.

And I thought of the wasps' nest in the bank
And how I got chased one day
Leaving the drag and the scraw-knife behind,
How I covered my face with hay.

The wet leaves of the cocksfoot
Polished my boots as I
Went round by the glistening bog-holes
Lost in unthinking joy.

I'll be carrying bags today, I mused,
the best job at the mill
With plenty of time to talk of our loves
As we wait for the bags to fill.

Maybe Mary might call round...
And then I came to the haggard gate,
And I knew as I entered that I had come
Through fields that were part of no earthly estate.

■ *Language and Concepts*

Mood
Mood is the feeling or emotion that the poet tries to convey in the
poem.

1   Write out as many different moods as you can, e.g. sorrowful, joyous. The class should be able to suggest up to thirty different moods.

2   What mood is the poet expressing in this poem? Be as accurate as possible — don't say 'a good mood' or 'a bad mood'.

3   The poet describes the morning as an 'apple-ripe September morning'. Go through each of the months of the year and try to find a word or phrase to go with each month.

4   How did Tarry Flynn expect to spend the day at the threshing?

5   'With work thrown in to ballast/The fantasy-soaring mind.' Have you ever worked at a job which, though hard, was enjoyable and fulfilling? Write a paragraph about it.

In Memory of My Mother

Patrick Kavanagh

I do not think of you lying in the wet clay
Of a Monaghan graveyard; I see
You walking down a lane among the poplars
On your way to the station, or happily

Going to second Mass on a summer Sunday —
You meet me and you say:
"Don't forget to see about the cattle — "
Among your earthiest words the angels stray.

And I think of you walking along a headland
Of green oats in June,
So full of repose, so rich with life —
And I see us meeting at the end of a town

On a fair day by accident, after
The bargains are all made and we can walk
Together through the shops and stalls and markets
Free in the oriental streets of thought.

O you are not lying in the wet clay,
For it is a harvest evening now and we
Are piling up the ricks against the moonlight
And you smile up at us — eternally.

■ *Language and Concepts*

Elegy
An elegy is a poem written in memory of somebody who has died.
It does not go over all the details of the dead person's life but
rather tries to convey what the dead person meant to the poet.

Obituary
An obituary usually appears in a newspaper just after somebody
has died. The obituary is like a brief biography which tries to give
a summary of the events of a person's life.

■ *Readings and Responses*

1 What memories of his mother does the poet still have in his
   mind?

2 'Among your earthiest words the angels stray.' What is meant
   by these words?

3 'Free in the oriental streets of thought.' What is meant by
   these words?

4 What kind of person do you think Kavanagh's mother was?
   Each verse gives us a clue to her personality.

A Christmas Childhood

Patrick Kavanagh

I

One side of the potato-pits was white with frost —
How wonderful that was, how wonderful!
And when we put our ears to the paling-post
The music that came out was magical.

The light between the ricks of hay and straw
Was a hole in Heaven's gable. An apple tree
With its December-glinting fruit we saw —
O you, Eve, were the world that tempted me

To eat the knowledge that grew in clay
And death the germ within it! Now and then
I can remember something of the gay
Garden that was childhood's. Again

The tracks of cattle to a drinking-place,
A green stone lying sideways in a ditch
Or any common sight the transfigured face
Of a beauty that the world did not touch.

II

My father played the melodeon
Outside at our gate;
There were stars in the morning east
And they danced to his music.

Across the wild bogs his melodeon called
To Lennons and Callans.
As I pulled on my trousers in a hurry
I knew some strange thing had happened.

Outside the cow-house my mother
Made the music of milking;
The light of her stable-lamp was a star
And the frost of Bethlehem made it twinkle.

A water-hen screeched in the bog,
Mass-going feet
Crunched the wafer-ice on the pot-holes,
Somebody wistfully twisted the bellows wheel.

My child poet picked out the letters
On the grey stone,
In silver the wonder of a Christmas townland,
The winking glitter of a frosty dawn.

Cassiopeia was over
Cassidy's hanging hill,
I looked and three whin bushes rode across
The horizon — the Three Wise Kings.

An old man passing said:
"Can't he make it talk" —
The melodeon. I hid in the doorway
And tightened the belt of my box-pleated coat.

I nicked six nicks on the door-post
With my penknife's big blade —
There was a little one for cutting tobacco.
And I was six Christmases of age.

My father played the melodeon,
My mother milked the cows,
And I had a prayer like a white rose pinned
On the Virgin Mary's blouse.

■ *Readings and Responses*

1   What two words, in the first verse, tell us how the child feels
    at Christmas?

2   'The light of her Stable-lamp was a star
    And the frost of Bethlehem made it twinkle.'
        and
    'I looked and three whin bushes rode across
    The horizon — the Three Wise Kings.'

    What do these lines tell us of how real the Christmas story is
    to the child?

3   Pick out lines which appeal to the different senses.

4   A major theme in this poem is the innocence of childhood.
    Pick out the lines and images which show this.

5   Write about Christmas under three or four headings. Try to
    avoid clichés.

Spraying the Potatoes

Patrick Kavanagh

The barrels of blue potato-spray
Stood on a headland of July
Beside an orchard wall where roses
Were young girls hanging from the sky.

The flocks of green potato-stalks
Were blossoms spread for sudden flight,
The Kerr's Pinks in a frivelled blue,
The Aran Banners wearing white.

And over that potato-field
A lazy veil of woven sun.
Dandelions growing on headlands, showing
Their unloved hearts to everyone.

And I was there with the knapsack sprayer
On the barrel's edge poised. A wasp was floating
Dead on a sunken briar leaf
Over a copper-poisoned ocean.

The axle-roll of a rut-locked cart
Broke the burnt stick of noon in two.
An old man came through a corn-field
Remembering his youth and some Ruth he knew.

He turned my way. "God further the work."
He echoed an ancient farming prayer.
I thanked him. He eyed the potato-drills.
He said: "You are bound to have good ones there."

We talked and our talk was a theme of kings,
A theme for strings. He hunkered down
In the shade of the orchard wall. O roses
The old man dies in the young girl's frown.

And poet lost to potato-fields,
Remembering the lime and copper smell
Of the spraying barrels he is not lost
Or till blossomed stalks cannot weave a spell.

Concrete language
The most powerful language will try to avoid generalisations, that is, referring to things in general rather than describing specific examples. When a description is particular and gives specific examples concrete language is used. Concrete language is the opposite of generalised language. You should try to use concrete language in your writing.

■ *Readings and Responses*

1   Pick out three specific examples of concrete details given by Kavanagh in the first four verses.

2   There are some very good visual images in the poem. Pick out two descriptions which you can see in your mind's eye.

3   Where in the poem is the theme of love referred to?

4   'Frivelled' is a word coined by Kavanagh. What does it suggest to you.

5   Describe the school playground using as much concrete language and details as you can.

THE LANGUAGE OF THE SENSES

■

In Pete Townsend's rock-opera *Tommy* there is a character, the pinball wizard, who is the world's greatest pinball player even though he is deaf, dumb and blind. As the words of the song says: 'He plays by intuition/Becomes part of the machine'.

The pinball wizard is operating under impossible handicaps because it is through our five senses — touch, sight, hearing, taste, smell — that we experience the world and it is through our language that our experiences are organised.

Poetry, because it is concerned with our experience of living, is at the meeting point of the senses and language. Many powerful poems make strong appeals to our five senses.

Annie's Song

Young Shepherd Bathing his Feet

Noise

I like that stuff

Snow

■

Annie's Song

John Denver

You fill up my senses
Like a night in a forest
Like the mountains in springtime
Like a walk in the rain
Like a storm in a desert
Like a sleepy blue ocean
You fill up my senses
Come fill me again.

Come let me love you
Let me give my life to you
Let me drown in your laughter
Let me die in your arms
Let me lay down beside you
Let me always be with you
Come let me love you, come love me again.

■ *Readings and Responses*

1   John Denver wants to describe the depth of his love so he
    says 'you fill up my senses'. He then thinks of five other
    experiences which 'fill up his senses'. Which of the five similes
    do you think is the best?

2   Take one of the similes and write a paragraph showing how it
    fills up the senses. Try to appeal to all the senses.

3   Can you add some more similes which fill up the senses?

4   Try to obtain a recording of this song either by John Denver
    or as played by James Galway.

5   Could this song have been put into the section on love in this
    book? Is it a good love song? Why?

Young Shepherd Bathing his Feet

Peter Clarke

Only the short, broad, splayed feet
Moved ...

Feet that had trodden over
Soft soil,
Sand,
Ploughed veld,
Mountain rocks
And along narrow tracks,
On Winter clay and
Dust of Summer roads ...

The short, broad, splayed feet
Moved
In and out ...

The stumpy toes stretched wide
Apart
And closed together
Then opened wide ...

In ecstasy.

■ *Readings and Responses*

1   Which word tells us of the sheer pleasure felt by the young
    shepherd as he is bathing his feet?

2   Why are his feet so weary?

3   Which sense is appealed to most strongly in this poem?

4   Which word do you think most vividly describes the
    appearance of the toes?

5   It is said that a person's hands can be very eloquent. Write a
    description of a hand which reveals something of the person
    whose hand it is.

Noise

Jessie Pope

I like noise.
The whoop of a boy, the thud of a hoof,
The rattle of rain on a galvanised roof,
The hubbub of traffic, the roar of a train,
The throb of machinery numbing the brain,
The switching of wires in an overhead tram,
The rush of the wind, a door on the slam,
The boom of the thunder, the crash of the waves,
The din of a river that races and raves,
The crack of a rifle, the clank of a pail,
The strident tattoo of a swift-slapping sail —
From any old sound that the silence destroys,
Arises a gamut of soul-stirring joys.
I like noise.

■ *Language and Concepts*

Precision of language
There are so many words in the English language that dictionaries can contain hundreds of thousands of different words. Each word has a different shade of meaning and each word has different connotations; each word suggests slightly different pictures in our mind. The aim of the good writer or poet is precision of language: he or she must search out precisely the right word and reject other words.

■ *Readings and Responses*

1 Which do you think is the most vivid and interesting noise in the poem?

2 Look at the following words: noise, sound, cacophony, harmony, commotion, blare, racket, hubbub, pandemonium, din. Can you detect a different shade of meaning in all these words? Write a sentence which illustrates this difference.

3 Make a list of at least five sounds or noises which you really like. Try to do this in a manner similar to the poet.

4 'The radio is better than the TV because the pictures are better.' Can you explain and justify this paradox?

I like that stuff

Adrian Mitchell

Lovers lie around in it.
Broken glass is found in it
Grass
I like that stuff

Tuna fish get wrapped in it
Legs come wrapped in it
Nylon
I like that stuff

Eskimos and tramps chew it
Madame Tussaud gave status to it
Wax
I like that stuff

Elephants get sprayed with it
Scotch is made with it
Water
I like that stuff

Clergy are dumbfounded by it
Bones are surrounded by it
Flesh
I like that stuff

Harps are strung with it
Mattresses are sprung with it
Wire
I like that stuff

Cigarettes are lit by it
Pensioners get happy when they sit by it
Fire
I like that stuff

Dankworth's alto is made of it, most of it,
Scoobdedoo is composed of it
Plastic
I like that stuff

Man made fibres and raw materials
Old rolled gold and breakfast cereals
Platinum linoleum
I like that stuff

Skin on my hands
Hair on my head
Toenails on my feet
And linen on my bed

Well I like that stuff
Yes I like that stuff
    The earth
Is made of earth
    And I like that stuff

■ *Language and Concepts*

Repeated patterns
Poets try to use language in the most powerful effective way they
can. They work on the sound of the words, the rhythm of the
words, repetition of words, the placement of words, the
suggestions made by words. Another technique used by poets is
that of repeating certain patterns. Study closely the verses in *I
like that stuff* and you will see that almost all the verses follow a
regular pattern. This patterning reinforces the ideas the poet
wishes to express. The repetition and patterning 'emphasises'
how much he likes 'that stuff'.

■ *Readings and Responses*

1   Which of the senses are appealed to in this poem? Point out
    examples.

2   Which is your favourite verse? Why?

3   Do you think this is a poem of celebration and joy? Why?

4   Work out how each verse is organised into a regular pattern.

5   Think of some things or activities you really like. Try to put
    them into some more verses with the same pattern as *I like
    that stuff.*

Snow

Louis MacNeice

The room was suddenly rich and the great bay-window was
Spawning snow and pink roses against it
Soundlessly collateral and incompatible:
World is suddener than we fancy it.

World is crazier and more of it than we think
Incorrigibly plural. I peel and portion
A tangerine and spit the pips and feel
The drunkenness of things being various.

And the fire flames with a bubbling sound for world
Is more spiteful and gay than one supposes —
On the tongue on the eyes on the ears in the palms of one's
    hands —
There is more than glass between the snow and the huge roses.

■ *Language and Concepts*

The Extraordinary in the Ordinary
Sometimes poets try to shock us into seeing the wonder of ordinary things. A great philosopher once said that the most amazing thing in the universe was the sheer fact of being alive at all. Our sense of wonder becomes dulled by everyday life. However, artists, such as poets and painters, seem to have a keener awareness of the wonderful, astonishing, awesome majesty of the world in which we live.

■ *Readings and Responses*

1   What two things which usually do not exist together does the poet see together in the first verse?

2   How many of the senses are appealed to in this poem? Point out examples.

3   'and feel/The drunkenness of things being various.'

Explain what is meant by these words. Do they sum up what the poem is about?

4   Can you think of any ordinary thing or activity which you feel is unappreciated? Write a paragraph about it.

5   What do you think of the title of this poem? (Can you suggest a better one?)

PAUL DURCAN

Paul Durcan was born in Dublin in 1944 of Co. Mayo parents. He attended University College, Cork. Paul Durcan gives very individual readings of his poems and his readings attract large audiences. He lives in Dublin.

November 1967

In Memory of those Murdered in the Dublin Massacre, May 1974

What is a Protestant, Daddy?

Backside to the wind

Stellar Manipulator

November 1967

to Katherine

Paul Durcan

I awoke with a pain in my head
And my mother standing at the end of the bed;
'There's bad news in the paper,' she said
'Patrick Kavanagh is dead.'

After a week which was not real
At last I settled down to a natural meal;
I was sitting over a pint and a beef sandwich
In Mooney's across the street from the Rotunda.

By accident I happened to tune in
To the conversation at the table from me;
I heard an old Northsider tell to his missus
'He was pure straight; God rest him; not like us.

■ *Language and Concepts*

Colloquial and Formal language
Colloquial language is the kind of language we might use in a conversation. Formal language is the kind of language found in business letters, documents, textbooks. Formal language excludes slang and dialect words whereas colloquial language may include these.

■ *Readings and Responses*

1   Is the language in this poem colloquial or formal? Support your answer by giving an example.

2   What is meant by the last line? Is it sometimes difficult, even impossible or wrong, to be 'pure straight'? Can life be especially difficult for somebody who is pure straight?

3   Paul Durcan often writes about ordinary, everyday life. Pick out some references to ordinary everyday life in this poem.

4   Would you describe this as a realistic poem? Why?

5   Do you notice that there are many rhymes in this poem? Does this seem surprising?

In Memory of Those Murdered in the Dublin Massacre, May 1974

Paul Durcan

In the grime-ridden sunlight in the downtown Wimpy bar
I think of all the crucial aeons — and of the labels
That freedom fighters stick onto the lost destinies of
unborn children;
The early morning sunlight carries in the whole street from
outside;
The whole wide street from outside through the plate-glass
windows;
Wholly, sparklingly, surgingly, carried in from outside;
And the waitresses cannot help but be happy and gay
As they swipe at the table-tops with their dishcloths —
Such a moment as would provide the heroic freedom fighter
With his perfect meat.
And I think of those heroes — heroes? — and how truly
Obscene is war.

And as I stand up to walk out —
The aproned old woman who's been sweeping the floor
Has mop stuck in bucket, leaning on it;
And she's trembling all over, like a flower in the breeze.
She'd make a mighty fine explosion now, if you were to
blow her up;
An explosion of petals, of aeons, and the waitresses too,
flying breasts and limbs,
For a free Ireland.

■ *Language and Concepts*

Irony
Irony exists when there is a contrast between the words said and some underlying meaning which is really meant. In this simple sense, irony is similar to sarcasm. If a class has done some very poor work for a teacher and the teacher says to the class, in a particular tone of voice, 'Oh yes, you are a wonderful class', the teacher is being ironical because there is a gap between what the words say on the surface and what is really meant — on the surface the words mean they are a good class, but the teacher really means they are not.

1   What is meant by 'the lost destinies of unborn children'?

2   What kind of a day is suggested by the words 'sparklingly, surgingly'?

3   What does the word 'meat' referring to a human being suggest about the 'freedom fighters'?

4   'She'd make a mighty fine explosion now.' In what tone of voice are these words meant to be said?

5   What are the different nuances of meaning conveyed by the words 'freedom fighter' 'terrorist', 'rebel', 'soldier'?

What is a Protestant, Daddy?

Paul Durcan

Gaiters were sinister
And you dared not
Glance up at the visage;
It was a long lean visage
With a crooked nose
And beaked dry lips
And streaky gray hair
And they used scurry about
In small black cars
(Unlike Catholic bishops
Stately in big cars
Or Pope Pius XII
In his gold-plated Cadillac)
And they'd make dashes for it
Across deserted streets
And disappear quickly
Into vast cathedrals
All silent and aloof,
Forlorn and leafless,
Their belfry louvres
Like dead men's lips,
And whose congregations, if any,
Were all octogenarian
With names like Iris;
More likely
There were no congregations

And these rodent-like clergymen
Were conspirators;
You could see it in their faces;
But as to what the conspiracies
Were about, as children
We were at a loss to know;
Our parents called them 'parsons'
Which turned them from being rodents
Into black hooded crows
Evilly flapping their wings
About our virginal souls;
And these 'parsons' had wives —
As unimaginable a state of affairs
As it would have been to imagine
A pope in a urinal;
Protestants were Martians
Light-years more weird
Than zoological creatures;
But soon they would all go away
For as a species they were dying out.
Soon there would be no more Protestants ...
O Yea, O Lord,
I was a proper little Irish Catholic boy
Way back in the 1950s.

■ *Readings and Responses*

1   What is suggested by the use of the word 'sinister' with regard to the Protestant clergyman?

2   Can you find examples of offensive words used about the clergymen in the poem?

3   Does the poet really mean that the clergymen were 'conspirators'?

4   What is the tone of the last two lines? Is there a contrast between what the words seem to say and what the poet really means?

5   Is there still prejudice present in Irish society in relation to minority groups. Write a paragraph on a particular minority group, e.g. the Travellers, the Jehovah's Witnesses, Protestants.

Backside to the wind

Paul Durcan

A fourteen-year-old boy is out rambling alone
By the scimitar shores of Killala Bay
And he is dreaming of a French Ireland
Backside to the wind.

What kind of village would I now be living in?
French vocabularies intertwined with Gaelic
And Irish women with French fathers
Backside to the wind.

The Ballina road would become the Rue de Humbert
And wine would be the staple drink of the people;
A staple diet of potatoes and wine
Backsides to the wind.

Monsieur O'Duffy might be the harbour-master
And Madame Duffy the mother of thirteen
Tiny philosophers to overthrow Maynooth
Backsides to the wind.

And Father Molloy might be a worker-priest
Up to his knees in manure at the cattle-mart;
And dancing and loving on the streets at evening
Backsides to the wind.

Jean Arthur Rimbaud might have grown up here
In a hillside terrace under the round tower;
Would he, like me, have dreamed of an Arabian Dublin
Backside to the wind?

And Garda Ned MacHale might now be a gendarme
Having hysterics at the crossroads;
Excommunicating male motorists, ogling females
Backsides to the wind.

I walk on, facing the village ahead of me,
A small concrete oasis in the wild countryside;
Not the embodiment of the dream of a boy
Backside to the wind.

Seagulls and crows, priests and nuns,
Perch on the rooftops and steeples,
And their Anglo-American mores are killing me
Backside to the wind.

Not to mention the Japanese invasion:
Blunt people as serious as ourselves
And as humourless; money is our God
Backsides to the wind.

The ancient Franciscan Friary of Moyne
Stands nobly, roofless, by;
Past it rolls a vast concrete pipe
Backside to the wind.

Carrying out chemical waste to sea
From the Asahi synthetic-fibre plant;
Where once monks sang, wage-earners slave
Backsides to the wind.

Yet somehow, sweet River Moy,
Run on though I end my song;
You are the vestments of the salmon of learning
Backside to the wind.

But I have no choice but to leave, to leave,
And yet there is nowhere I more yearn to live
Than in my own wild countryside
Backside to the wind.

■ *Readings and Responses*

1 The boy tries to imagine what would have happened if the
   French, who arrived in Killala in 1798, had stayed and Ireland
   had come under French influence. Show how the poet
   extracts humour from the new combination of Irish and
   French characteristics.

2 What contrast does the poet draw between the friary at Moyne
   and the Asahi factory?

3 President Mary Robinson in her inaugural address quoted the
   last verse of this poem when she was lamenting emigration.
   Explain what is meant by the last verse.

4 Would you say that the poet has a love/hate relationship with
   Ireland? Support your answer by precise reference to lines
   from the poem.

5 Write down the five things you would most miss if you left
   Ireland.

Stellar Manipulator

Paul Durcan

I
Judge Durcan, you wanted
Your eldest son to be a lawyer.
But wanting always to be
Like the other you, Daddy,
To become your understudy,
I became at the age of twenty-five
Stellar Manipulator
At the London Planetarium.

When I went for the interview
With the Director of the Planetarium,
John Ebdon,
He so much looked
And sounded like you
I had to be careful not
To address him as Daddy.
'I hear that you write
Poetry' — he exclaimed.
I winced. He continued:
Many a night I saw the Pleiads,
    rising through the mellow shade,
Glitter like a swarm of fire-flies
    tangled in a silver braid.
When I failed to identify
The author, he said
'Tennyson' — and gave me the job.

II
Seven a.m. on a black Sunday morning
In Ladbroke Grove.
The black telephone. Your black voice.
'This is Harrow Road Police Station:
You are requested to act as bailsman.'
Down at the station at 7.45 a.m.
The duty officer takes down details.
Status: Married. *Sex*: Male.
Nationality: Irish. *Age*: 25.
Occupation: Stellar Manipulator.
The duty officer focuses his eyes
And asks me to repeat my occupation
That he can note it down correctly.

I say it with deliberation,
Pronouncing solemnly each syllable:
'Stell-ar Man-ip-ul-at-or.'
He smiles as you used smile, Daddy,
If ever there was so much as the remotest
Rumour of humour in the universe,
A smidgen of light in the black.

III
Back home in Dublin
In the locker room of the golf club,
When other members of the fourball
Enquire after your eldest son,
Knowing that I am the black
Sheep of the family,
Thinking to get a rise out of you,
'Well, what's he working at now?'
You take your time,
Scrutinising the clay adhering
To the studs of your golf shoes,
Scraping it off with a penknife.
Laconic, offhand:
'He's a—' satisfactorily
Flaking off another lump of clay,
'Stellar Manipulator'.

■ *Language and Concepts*

Euphemism

When it is wished to say not too bluntly or too directly what is
meant, a euphemism is used, e.g.
dustman — refuse collection officer
kill — eliminate; liquidate
died — passed away
lie — terminological inexactitude
civilian deaths — collateral damage

■ *Readings and Responses*

1   Was Judge Durcan pleased that his son obtained a job using a
    machine to move the artificial stars in the London Palladium?

2   Why does the poet keep emphasising that he is a 'stellar
    manipulator'? Is he being sarcastic?

3   What does the poet suggest by referring to the 'black voice' of
    his father?

4   Can you think of any euphemisms? Think perhaps of
    language used in war by governments to hide the killing.

EVERYBODY IS UNIQUE

■

Every human being is special — a unique, once-off individual: there never was or there never will be the same again. We all have our own identities, our own beliefs, our own experiences. Each of the characters presented in this section is memorable in his or her own way.

The Old Woman of the Roads

What Has Happened to Lulu?

The weepies

Colonel Frazackerley

The Unknown Citizen To JS/07/M378

Eleanor Rigby

'All the world's a stage'

Last days in the Party

■

The Old Woman of the Roads

Padraic Colum

O, to have a little house!
    To own the hearth and stool and all!
The heaped-up sods upon the fire,
    The pile of turf against the wall!

To have a clock with weights and chains
    And pendulum swinging up and down!
A dresser filled with shining delph,
    Speckled and white and blue and brown!

I could be busy all the day
    Clearing and sweeping hearth and floor
And fixing on their shelf again
    My white and blue and speckled store!

I could be quiet there at night,
    Beside the fire and by myself,
Sure of a bed; and loth to leave
    The ticking clock and the shining delph!

Oh! but I'm weary of mist and dark,
    And roads where there's never a house or bush,
And tired I am of the bog, and the road,
    And the crying wind and the lonesome hush!

And I am praying to God on high,
    And I am praying Him night and day,
For a little house — a house of my own —
    Out of the wind's and the rain's way.

■ *Readings and Responses*

1 How would you most accurately describe the mood expressed
in this poem: longing, weariness, misery, despair, hope,
optimism? Give reasons for your answer by pointing to
evidence from the poem.

2 The senses of sight, hearing and touch are appealed to in this
poem. In the case of each of these senses pick out a line
which appeals to it.

3 'And the crying wind and the lonesome hush'. What sound is
suggested by the long vowel sounds of this line?

4 The old woman says she is praying to God. Could this poem
be seen as her prayer? Explain.

What Has Happened to Lulu?

Charles Causley

What has happened to Lulu, mother?
  What has happened to Lu?
There's nothing in her bed but an old rag doll
  And by its side a shoe.

Why is her window wide, mother,
  The curtain flapping free,
And only a circle on the dusty shelf
  Where her money-box used to be?

Why do you turn your head, mother,
  And why do the tear-drops fall?
And why do you crumple that note on the fire
  And say it is nothing at all?

I woke to voices late last night,
  I heard an engine roar.
Why do you tell me the things I heard
  Were a dream and nothing more?

I heard somebody cry, mother,
  In anger or in pain,
But now I ask you why, mother,
  You say it was a gust of rain.

Why do you wander about as though
  You don't know what to do?
What has happened to Lulu, mother?
  What has happened to Lu?

 Language and Concepts

Point of view

A story or an incident which happens can appear totally different
to different participants. Let us take the example of a car accident
involving a drunken driver and a bus carrying young children.
The drunken driver, the driver of the bus, the young children in
the bus and an adult bystander will all have different reactions to
the accident. The truth of a story depends to a certain extent on
every point of view, not necessarily because anybody is telling
lies, but because no one person can see the full picture: they tell
the story from their point of view.

■ *Readings and Responses*

1   Who is speaking in this poem? From whose point of view is the story revealed?

2   There are clues throughout the poem which provide hints to tell us what Lulu has done. What are they?

3   Does the speaker in this poem understand the hints? Does he or she feel something different has happened? What is the effect of all the questions?

4   What is the mother's reaction to Lulu's departure? Is she trying to protect the child who is speaking?

5   Tell Lulu's story from Lulu's point of view.

The weepies

Paul Muldoon

Most Saturday afternoons
At the local Hippodrome
Saw the Pathe-News rooster,
Then the recurring dream

Of a lonesome drifter
Through uninterrupted range.
Will Hunter, so gifted
He could peel an orange

In a single, fluent gesture,
Was the leader of our gang.
The curtain rose this afternoon
On a lion, not a gong.

When the crippled girl
Who wanted to be a dancer
Met the married man
Who was dying of cancer,

Our hankies unfurled
Like flags of surrender.
I believe something fell asunder
In even Will Hunter's hands.

■ *Language and Concepts*

Stereotype

A stereotype is a typical example or representative. A stereo-typical 'bad guy' in a Western film might be unshaven, dressed in black and with a scowl on his face. A stereotypical gangster might have a pinstripe suit, a brightly coloured tie, a scar on his face and be driving a large American car.

■ *Readings and Responses*

1 What kind of films were usually shown on Saturday afternoons? Look at the beginning of the second verse for a stereotypical character.

2 Will Hunter's character is only suggested to us; nevertheless, what kind of boy do you think he was?

3 'Sentimental' means 'almost too full of emotion'. Do you think the film described in verse four was sentimental?

4 Why is Will Hunter's and his friend's reaction seen as a surrender? Were they as tough as they liked to pretend?

5 What film have you seen which had the most lasting effect on you?

Colonel Fazackerley

Charles Causley

Colonel Fazackerley Butterworth-Toast
Bought an old castle complete with a ghost,
But someone or other forgot to declare
To Colonel Fazack that the spectre was there.

On the very first evening, while waiting to dine,
The Colonel was taking a fine sherry wine,
When the ghost, with a furious flash and a flare,
Shot out of the chimney and shivered, 'Beware!'

Colonel Fazackerley put down his glass
And said, 'My dear fellow, that's really first class!
I just can't conceive how you do it at all.
I imagine you're going to a Fancy Dress Ball?'

At this, the dread ghost gave a withering cry.
Said the Colonel (his monocle firm in his eye),
'Now just how you do it I wish I could think.
Do sit down and tell me, and please have a drink.'

The ghost in his phosphorous cloak gave a roar
And floated about between ceiling and floor.
He walked through a wall and returned through a pane
And backed up the chimney and came down again.

Said the Colonel, 'With laughter I'm feeling quite weak!'
(As trickles of merriment ran down his cheek).
'My house-warming party I hope you won't spurn,
You must say you'll come and you'll give us a turn!'

At this, the poor spectre — quite out of his wits —
Proceeded to shake himself almost to bits.
He rattled his chains and he clattered his bones
And he filled the whole castle with mumbles and moans.

But Colonel Fazackerley, just as before,
Was simply delighted and called out, 'Encore!'
At which the ghost vanished, his efforts in vain,
And never was seen at the castle again.

'Oh dear, what a pity!' said Colonel Fazack.
'I don't know his name, so I can't call him back.'
And then with a smile that was hard to define,
Colonel Fazackerley went in to dine.

■ *Readings and Responses*

1   What do you think of Colonel Fazackerley's full name?

2   Describe what you think Colonel Fazackerley looks like.

3   What is the Colonel's reaction to the appearance of the spectre?

4   The spectre is completely confused. Why? How does he show his confusion?

5   Tell a ghost story making it as creepy and eerie as possible.

The Unknown Citizen To JS/07/M378

This marble monument is erected by the state

W.H. Auden

He was found by the Bureau of Statistics to be
One against whom there was no official complaint,
And all the reports on his conduct agree
That, in the modern sense of an old-fashioned word, he was
     a saint,
For in everything he did he served the Greater Community.
Except for the War till the day he retired
He worked in a factory and never got fired,
But satisfied his employers, Fudge Motors Inc.
Yet he wasn't a scab or odd in his views,
For his Union reports that he paid his dues,
(Our report on his Union shows it was sound)
And our Social Psychology workers found
That he was popular with his mates and liked a drink.
The Press are convinced that he bought a paper every day
And that his reactions to advertisements were normal in every
     way.
Policies taken out in his name prove that he was fully insured,
And his Health-card shows he was once in hospital but left
     it cured.

Both Producers Research and High-Grade Living declare
He was fully sensible to the advantages of the Instalment
        Plan
And had everything necessary to the Modern Man,
A phonograph, a radio, a car and a frigidaire.
Our researchers into Public Opinion are content
That he held the proper opinions for the time of year;
When there was peace, he was for peace; when there was war,
        he went.
He was married and added five children to the population,
Which our Eugenist says was the right number for a parent of
        his generation,
And our teachers report that he never interfered with their
        education.
Was he free? Was he happy? The question is absurd:
Had anything been wrong, we should certainly have heard.

■ *Language and Concepts*

Names

Everybody has a name; every place has a name. Up to recent
times farmers had different names for all their fields (Has this
practice ceased and if it has does it tell us anything about the
environmental crisis?). People name animals. To name something
is to say something about its identity. Our names provide us with
a mark of our uniqueness. Parents go to great trouble naming
their children. Friends have nicknames for one another. Parents
and lovers sometimes have pet-names for their loved ones.

■ *Readings and Responses*

1   What is the significance of the fact that The Unknown
    Citizen's name is JS/07/M378?

2   The Unknown Citizen is popular, works hard, holds the usual
    opinions. Why is his life very 'inhuman' and 'poverty-
    stricken'?

3   What kind of language is used in this poem? Give some
    examples. Where is this kind of language normally used? Who
    is speaking in this poem?

4   'Was he free? Was he happy? The question is absurd.'

    Why are these the most 'dehumanised' words in the poem? If
    human beings are not 'free' in what sense are they still
    human?

5   Write an essay on 'Names of people and places'.

Eleanor Rigby

John Lennon and Paul McCartney

Ah, look at all the lonely people! Ah, look at all the lonely people!
Eleanor Rigby picks up the rice in the church where a wedding
   has been,
Lives in a dream, Waits at the window, wearing the face that she
   keeps in a jar by the door.
Who is it for? All the lonely people, where do they all come from?
All the lonely people, where do they all belong?

Father McKenzie, writing the words of a sermon that no one will
   hear.
No one comes near. Look at him working, darning his socks in
   the night
When there's nobody there. What does he care? All the lonely
   people,
Where do they all come from? All the lonely people, where do they
   all belong?

Eleanor Rigby died in the church and was buried along with her
   name. Nobody came.
Father McKenzie wiping the dirt from his hands as he walks from
   the grave. No one was saved ...
All the lonely people, Where do they all come from? All the lonely
   people, where do they all belong?

■ *Language and concepts*

Popular songs

The words of some popular songs can be powerful and vivid. Two such are included in this book, *Eleanor Rigby* by Lennon and McCartney and *Annie's Song* by John Denver. In some popular songs the words are not regarded as important; the beat and the rhythm of the melody are much more resonant. In those songs the words can be very thin and lacking in punch. Listen to the words of the songs as well as to the music because some pop artists have poetic talent.

■ *Readings and Responses*

1   Why is it particularly sad that Eleanor Rigby should be on her own when there has just been a wedding?

2   Why is Father McKenzie so isolated?

3   What is the most vivid picture created in this song?

4   Write another verse choosing two or three significant details from the life of another lonely person.

5   Try to obtain a recording of this song and play it for the class.

'All the world's a stage'

William Shakespeare

From *As You Like It*, Act 2 Scene 7

All the world's a stage,
And all the men and women merely players:
They have their exits and their entrances;
And one man in his time plays many parts,
His acts being seven ages. At first the infant,
Mewling and puking in the nurse's arms.
And then the whining schoolboy, with his satchel,
And shining morning face, creeping like snail
Unwillingly to school. And then the lover,
Sighing like furnace, with a woeful ballad
Made to his mistress' eyebrow. Then a soldier,
Full of strange oaths, and bearded like the pard,
Jealous in honour, sudden and quick in quarrel,
Seeking the bubble reputation
Even in the cannon's mouth. And then the justice,
In fair round belly with good capon lin'd,
With eyes severe, and beard of formal cut,
Full of wise saws and modern instances;
And so he plays his part. The sixth age shifts
Into the lean and slipper'd pantaloon,
With spectacles on nose and pouch on side,
His youthful hose well sav'd, a world too wide
For his shrunk shank; and his big manly voice,
turning again toward childish treble, pipes
And whistles in his sound. Last scene of all,
That ends this strange eventful history,
Is second childishness and mere oblivion,
Sans teeth, sans eyes, sans taste, sans everything.

■ *Readings and Responses*

1   Shakespeare was an actor for most of his life and he often compared the world to a stage. Is it true that for much of our lives we have to play different parts or roles? Do we, for example, play a role when we are talking to the Principal of the school different to the role we play when talking to our friends? Explain your answer.

2   Divide up the seven ages of man, e.g. the infant 1-4 and so on.

3 Which of the seven ages do you think Shakespeare has
described most vividly?

4 What is meant by 'mewling', the 'bubble reputation', and
'mere oblivion'?

5 How would you describe the view of life presented in this
speech: sad, tragic, realistic, true?

Last days in the Party

Thomas McCarthy

You let the razor-wound bleed in the warm
Wet silence. In the stains on your bright
Shirt I could gauge developing sorrows:
Earlier, you had forgotten the discussion
Papers, abandoned them in the locked car
As if they were blood-hardened criminals.

You planned to leave with dignity: after
Years of election committees and country
Meetings you had hoped for an after-glow
Of respect, a friendly exchange of roles:
Instead, you discovered a packed meeting,
Delegates like matadors waiting for blood.

Ten years ago you brought me to the first
Conference. Then you handled words calmly,
Juggled with complaints from the platform,
Tied hostilities neatly on a long string
Of language. Trapped in that jungle of old
Men, I made a beacon of your word-play.

Tonight, Father, master of tough language,
It's you I find trapped on a tightening
Syntax; pulled out of depth. The young man
In the trendy suit laughs when he takes
Your place. His broad smile is your dead
Old cheer; a flourish without permanence.

 Language and Concepts

Political language
Politicians have to be masters of language not just because they
have to make so many speeches, but because they have to be
able to explain, persuade, encourage, inspire and convince.
Politicians, like poets, must be aware of all the nuances of words
and all their shades of meaning.

 Readings and Responses

1   Tell the story of this poem.

2   The poet's father had been a master of political language.
    Look at the third verse. How is this mastery shown?

3   What image is used in the first three lines of the last verse?

4   Does this poem show that politics can be very cruel and
    unfeeling? Explain your answer.

5   Prepare a talk or write an essay about your favourite
    politician.

W.B. YEATS

∎

W.B. Yeats was born in Dublin in 1865. His family originated in Sligo. Early in his career he was influenced by folktales and ancient Irish mythology. He fell in love with Maud Gonne who was the daughter of an English army officer. He wrote many love poems to her over a long period of time. Yeats founded the Irish National Theatre. In 1923 he won the Nobel prize for literature. He died in 1939 and is buried in Drumcliffe, Co. Sligo. He is regarded as one of the greatest writers of the twentieth century.

The Lake Isle of Innisfree

He Wishes for the Cloths of Heaven

To a Child Dancing in the Wind

The Wild Swans at Coole

A Prayer for my Daughter

∎

The Lake Isle of Innisfree

W.B. Yeats

I will arise and go now, and go to Innisfree,
And a small cabin build there, of clay and wattles made;
Nine bean rows will I have there, a hive for the honey bee,
    And live alone in the bee-loud glade.

And I shall have some peace there, for peace comes dropping slow,
Dropping from the veils of the morning to where the cricket sings;
There midnight's all a glimmer, and noon a purple glow,
    And evening full of the linnet's wings.

I will arise and go now, for always night and day
I hear lake water lapping with low sounds by the shore;
While I stand on the roadway, or on the pavements gray,
    I hear it in the deep heart's core.

■ *Language and Concepts*

Idyll
An idyll is a short poem presenting a happy, pleasant scene in rural surroundings. The scene presented is 'idyllic' or perfect. Yeats, when he wrote the poem above, was living in London and he remembers a scene from his visits to Sligo. He then creates this idyllic picture of rural life to contrast with the 'pavements gray' of London.

■ *Readings and Responses*

1   When you have read the poem a number of times think of a precise word to describe the mood of the poet.

2   In this poem there is a particular appeal to the aural sense. Pick out two vivid examples.

3   There is very effective use of alliteration and onomatopoeia in the last verse. Pick it out and say what image it creates in your mind.

4   Is it fair to say that this is an 'escapist' poem; that the poet is trying to escape from reality into a dream world?

5   Write a paragraph describing the most beautiful place you have ever seen. Try to appeal to the senses of the reader by your words.

He Wishes for the Cloths of Heaven

W.B. Yeats

Yeats was hopelessly in love with Maud Gonne for many years and he wrote about her obsessively. She was the daughter of an English army colonel and she became an extreme Irish nationalist. *He Wishes for the Cloths of Heaven* is one of the many poems Yeats wrote about her.

> Had I the heavens' embroidered cloths,
> Enwrought with golden and silver light,
> The blue and the dim and the dark cloths
> Of night and light and the half-light,
> I would spread the cloths under your feet:
> But I, being poor, have only my dreams;
> I have spread my dreams under your feet;
> Tread softly because you tread on my dreams.

■ *Readings and Responses*

1   How might this poem bring to mind the story of Sir Walter Raleigh laying his cloak on the puddle of water before Queen Elizabeth?

2   What are the 'heavens' embroidered cloths' which he is going to lay under her feet?

3   What is meant by the line:

'Tread softly because you tread on my dreams'?

4   Does this poem convey the extent and depth of Yeats' love for Maud Gonne?

5   Do you notice that this poem contains none of the clichés associated with love-songs? Can you recall any such clichés from popular songs?

To a Child Dancing in the Wind
W.B. Yeats

Dance there upon the shore;
What need have you to care
For wind or water's roar?
And tumble out your hair
That the salt drops have wet;
Being young you have not known
The fool's triumph, nor yet
Love lost as soon as won,
Nor the best labourer dead
And all the sheaves to bind.
What need have you to dread
The monstrous crying of wind?

■ *Language and Concepts*

Innocence and maturity of knowledge
Living in the world means that we gain in experience day by day. Almost all stories are about this learning or movement from innocence to knowledge. In this poem Yeats is keenly aware of his own knowledge of the troubles of the world and of the child's innocence. The child is Maud Gonne's daughter Iseult. Some years later when Maud Gonne turned down yet another proposal of marriage from Yeats he then proposed to Iseult who also did not accept.

■ *Readings and Responses*

1   Why doesn't the child care about the 'wind or water's roar' or the 'monstrous crying of wind'?

2   What is meant by the 'fool's triumph'?

3   What is the difference between the child's attitude to the world and the poet's attitude?

4   Does the poet feel sorry for the child or does he envy her, or both?

5   What view of life is presented in this poem: realistic, pessimistic, gloomy, tragic? Give your reasons.

The Wild Swans at Coole

W.B. Yeats

The setting for this poem is Coole Park, near Gort, the home of
Lady Gregory whom Yeats often visited. He admired the gracious
lifestyle of the aristocratic Anglo-Irish who lived in the great
houses.

The trees are in their autumn beauty,
The woodland paths are dry,
Under the October twilight the water
Mirrors a still sky;
Upon the brimming water among the stones
Are nine-and-fifty swans.

The nineteenth autumn has come upon me
Since I first made my count;
I saw, before I had well finished,
All suddenly mount
And scatter wheeling in great broken rings
Upon their clamorous wings.

I have looked upon those brilliant creatures,
And now my heart is sore.
All's changed since I, hearing at twilight,
The first time on this shore,
The bell-beat of their wings above my head,
Trod with a lighter tread.

Unwearied still, lover by lover,
They paddle in the cold
Companionable streams or climb the air;
Their hearts have not grown old;
Passion or conquest, wander where they will,
Attend upon them still.

But now they drift on the still water,
Mysterious, beautiful;
Among what rushes will they build,
By what lake's edge or pool
Delight men's eyes when I awake some day
To find they have flown away?

1   What wonderfully clear and vivid picture does Yeats create in the first verse? Is it significant that it is autumn?

2   There are two fine aural images in verses two and three. Pick them out.

3   The poet's heart is 'sore'. Why? Look at verse three.

4   In what sense are the swans different to the poet? Look at verse four.

5   What is suggested to your mind by the line 'Mysterious, beautiful'?

A Prayer for my Daughter

W.B. Yeats

Once more the storm is howling, and half hid
Under this cradle-hood and coverlid
My child sleeps on. There is no obstacle
But Gregory's wood and one bare hill
Whereby the haystack- and roof-levelling wind,
Bred on the Atlantic, can be stayed;
And for an hour I have walked and prayed
Because of the great gloom that is in my mind.

I have walked and prayed for this young child an hour
And heard the sea-wind scream upon the tower,
And under the arches of the bridge, and scream
In the elms above the flooded stream;
Imagining in excited reverie
That the future years had come,
Dancing to a frenzied drum,
Out of the murderous innocence of the sea.

May she be granted beauty and yet not
Beauty to make a stranger's eye distraught,
Or hers before a looking-glass, for such,
Being made beautiful overmuch,
Consider beauty a sufficient end,
Lose natural kindness and maybe
The heart-revealing intimacy
That chooses right, and never find a friend.

Helen being chosen found life flat and dull
And later had much trouble from a fool,
While that great Queen, that rose out of the spray,
Being fatherless could have her way
Yet chose a bandy-legged smith for man.
It's certain that fine women eat
A crazy salad with their meat
Whereby the Horn of Plenty is undone.

In courtesy I'd have her chiefly learned;
Hearts are not had as a gift but hearts are earned
By those that are not entirely beautiful;
Yet many, that have played the fool
For beauty's very self, has charm made wise,
And many a poor man that has roved,
Loved and thought himself beloved,
From a glad kindness cannot take his eyes.

May she become a flourishing hidden tree
That all her thoughts may like the linnet be,
And have no business but dispensing round
Their magnanimities of sound,
Nor but in merriment begin a chase,
Nor but in merriment a quarrel.
O may she live like some green laurel
Rooted in one dear perpetual place.

My mind, because the minds that I have loved,
The sort of beauty that I have approved,
Prosper but little, has dried up of late,
Yet knows that to be choked with hate
May well be of all evil chances chief.
If there's no hatred in a mind
Assault and battery of the wind
Can never tear the linnet from the leaf.

An intellectual hatred is the worst,
So let her think opinions are accursed.
Have I not seen the loveliest woman born
Out of the mouth of Plenty's horn,
Because of her opinionated mind
Barter that horn and every good
By quiet natures understood
For an old bellows full of angry wind?

Considering that, all hatred driven hence,
The soul recovers radical innocence
And learns at last that it is self-delighting,

Self-appeasing, self-affrighting,
And that its own sweet will is Heaven's will;
She can, though every face should scowl
And every windy quarter howl
Or every bellows burst, be happy still.

And may her bridegroom bring her to a house
Where all's accustomed, ceremonious;
For arrogance and hatred are the wares
Peddled in the thoroughfares,
How but in custom and in ceremony
Are innocence and beauty born?
Ceremony's a name for the rich horn,
And custom for the spreading laurel tree.

■ *Readings and Responses*

1   Yeats' daughter, Anne, had recently been born. Read verse one. What occurs on this particular night which generates fear for his daughter in the mind of Yeats?

2   In verse two the poet has a kind of nightmare vision of the future. What kind of future is suggested by:

    'Dancing to a frenzied drum
    Out of the murderous innocence of the sea'?

3   In the third and fourth verses he expresses the hope that his daughter might be beautiful but not too beautiful. Why?

4   'fine women eat/A crazy salad with their meat.'

    What do these lines mean?

5   The eighth verse refers to Maud Gonne. What does Yeats say about her extreme nationalism?

6   Yeats' love of tradition and his ideal of the aristocratic life is expressed in the last verse. Describe the kind of life he sees as ideal for his daughter.

EPIPHANIES/MOMENTS OF INSIGHT

■

Epiphanies are special moments, moments of insight, utterly memorable moments when we seem to see life more clearly and with deeper understanding. We all experience such moments and we should treasure them as confirming our unique individuality.

Landscape with figures

The Caravels

Sonnet: On First Looking into Chapman's Homer

Stopping by Woods on a Snowy Evening

God's Grandeur

Miracles

Snaring

Skating

■

Landscape with figures

Frank Ormsby

What haunts me is a farmhouse among trees
Seen from a bus window, a girl
With a suitcase climbing a long hill
And a woman waiting.
The time the bus took to reach and pass
The lane's entrance nothing was settled,
The girl still climbing and the woman still
On the long hill's summit.

Men were not present. Neither in the fields
That sloped from hedges, nor beyond the wall
That marked the yard's limits
Was there sign of hens, or hands working.
No sight that might have softened
On the eye the scene's
Relentlessness.

Nothing had happened, yet the minute spoke
And the scene spoke and the silence,
And oppressed as air does, loading
For a storm's release.

All lanes and houses
Secretive in trees and gaunt hills' jawlines
Turn my thoughts again
To that day's journey and the thing I saw
And could not fathom. Struck with the same dread
I seem to share in sense, not detail,
What was heavy there:
Sadness of dim places, obscure lives,
Ends and beginnings,
Such extremities.

■ *Readings and Responses*

1   What scene haunts the poet?

2   'Sadness of dim places, obscure lives.' What does the poet mean by this?

3   'Nothing had happened, yet the minute spoke

And the scene spoke'

Why do you think the 'minute spoke' and 'the scene spoke'?

4   'loading/For a storm's release.'

What does this image suggest about what might happen?

5   Write the story of the girl's life.

The Caravels

(The Discovery)

Sir John Squire

There was an Indian, who had known no change,
Who strayed content along a sunlit beach
Gathering shells. He heard a sudden strange
Commingled noise; looked up; and gasped for speech.
For in the bay, where nothing was before,
Moved on the sea, by magic, huge canoes,
With bellying cloths on poles, and not one oar,
And fluttering coloured signs and clambering crews.

And he, in fear, this naked man alone,
His fallen hands forgetting all their shells,
His lips gone pale, knelt low behind a stone
And stared, and saw, and did not understand,
Columbus's doom-burdened caravels
Slant to the shore, and all their seamen land.

■ *Language and concepts*

A dramatic scene
The word 'drama' can have two meanings. Firstly, a drama is a play performed on stage; secondly 'drama' means something exciting or tense. A dramatic scene is created in our minds when an exciting, tense or thrilling event is described.

■ *Readings and Responses*

1   From whose point of view do we see the arrival of the ship (lines five — eight)? Look particularly at the words used to describe the sailing ships.

2   Notice how the first three lines have a smooth relaxed rhythm. Does the rhythm change in the fourth line? Why?

3   If you were to paint a picture of the scene described in the poem, what significant details would you concentrate on?

4   What is meant by 'doom-burdened caravels'?

5   'We have no right to force our beliefs and ways of life on other cultures.' Prepare a talk or write an essay on this topic.

Sonnet: On First Looking into Chapman's Homer

John Keats

Much have I travelled in the realms of gold,
   And many goodly states and kingdoms seen;
   Round many western islands have I been
Which bards in fealty to Apollo hold.
Oft of one wide expanse had I been told
   That deep-browed Homer ruled as his demesne;
   Yet did I never breathe its pure serene
Till I heard Chapman speak out loud and bold:

Then felt I like some watcher of the skies
   When a new planet swims into his ken;
Or like stout Cortez when with eagle eyes
   He stared at the Pacific — and all his men
Looked at each other with a wild surmise —
   Silent, upon a peak in Darien.

Chapman was an Elizabethan writer who translated Homer's great epic poems The Iliad and The Odyssey into English. Apollo is the Greek God of poetry and music.

■ *Readings and Responses*

1   The first eight lines (octave) of this sonnet are about Keats' reading. In what terms does he describe his reading?

2   In the sestet (the last six lines) Keats compares his discovery of Chapman's Homer to two other activities. What are they?

3   Is the placing of the word 'Silent' important? Why?

4   What aspects of the sonnet form are present in this poem? Look at the number of lines, the division into two parts and the rhyming scheme?

5   Name the book, film, poem or play that has most meaning for you. Say why you chose it.

Stopping by Woods on a Snowy Evening

Robert Frost

Whose woods these are I think I know.
His house is in the village though;
He will not see me stopping here
To watch his woods fill up with snow.

My little horse must think it queer
To stop without a farmhouse near
Between the woods and frozen lake
The darkest evening of the year.

He gives his harness bells a shake
To ask if there is some mistake.
The only other sound's the sweep
Of easy wind and downy flake.

The woods are lovely, dark and deep
But I have promises to keep,
And miles to go before I sleep,
And miles to go before I sleep.

■ *Readings and Responses*

1 One particular moment in time is isolated in this poem. Briefly describe this moment.

2 Why doesn't the horseman go to visit his friend in the village?

3 Read the poem aloud in the tone of voice which suits the meaning of the poem. Find one word to describe precisely the atmosphere created in the poem.

4 What kind of language is used in this poem?

5 Could this poem have a symbolic as well as a literal meaning? If so, what might the woods, the journey and the promises stand for?

God's Grandeur

Gerard Manley Hopkins

The world is charged with the grandeur of God.
  It will flame out, like shining from shook foil;
  It gathers to a greatness, like the ooze of oil
Crushed. Why do men then now not reck his rod?
Generations have trod, have trod, have trod;
  And all is seared with trade; bleared, smeared with toil:
  And wears man's smudge and shares man's smell: the soil
Is bare now, nor can foot feel, being shod.

And for all this, nature is never spent;
  There lives the dearest freshness deep down things;
And though the last lights off the black West went
  Oh, morning, at the brown brink eastward, springs —
Because the Holy Ghost over the bent
  World broods with warm breast and with ah! bright wings.

■ *Language and Concepts*

Word Choice and Word Placement
A poet, and indeed any writer, must search for the most exact, the most powerful words to convey his/her meaning. The placement of a word can also be important. Placing a word at the very opening of a poem can set the scene, evoke the mood, create the atmosphere, convey the theme of the poem. A word standing on its own can also be powerful. A word placed at the beginning of a line like the word 'Crushed' in *God's Grandeur* can also be effective because your attention is drawn to it.

■ *Readings and Responses*

1 There is a clearly defined idea in the octave and a new treatment of the idea in the sestet of this sonnet. What is the idea and the development?

2 What is the effect of the repetition in line five?

3 Pick out the assonance and internal alliteration in line six.

4 The mood of the poem is ultimately hopeful. Why?

5 Gerard Manley Hopkins, an English Jesuit priest, wrote this poem over a hundred years ago. One hundred years later, with the growth of environmental awareness, do you think its theme of the beauty and wonder of the world is still very relevant? Why?

Miracles

Walt Whitman

Why, who makes much of a miracle?
As to me I know of nothing else but miracles,
Whether I walk the streets of Manhattan,
Or dart my sight over the roofs of houses toward the sky,
Or wade with naked feet along the beach just in the edge
      of the water,
Or stand under trees in the woods,

Or sit at table at dinner with the rest,
Or look at strangers opposite me riding in the car,
Or watch honey-bees busy around the hive of a summer
      forenoon,
Or animals feeding in the fields,
Or birds, or the wonderfulness of insects in the air,
Or the wonderfulness of the sundown, or of stars shining so
      quiet and bright,
Or the exquisite delicate thin curve of the new moon in
      spring;
These with the rest, one and all, are to me miracles,
The whole referring, yet each distinct and in its place.

To me every hour of the light and dark is a miracle,
Every cubic inch of space is a miracle,
Every square yard of the surface of the earth is spread with
      the same,
Every foot of the interior swarms with the same.

To me the sea is a continual miracle,
The fishes that swim — the rocks — the motion of the waves —
      the ships with men in them,
What stranger miracles are there?

■ *Readings and Responses*

1   Which particular example of a miracle is most convincing and vivid? (One in particular seems to stand out.)

2   'The whole referring, yet each distinct and in its place.' Explain what is meant by this.

3   How would you describe the language of this poem?

4   The U.S.A. has been known as 'the land of opportunity'. Does this poem support this positive view of the U.S.A.?

5   Add some more lines of your own to this poem presenting what you think are miracles in everyday life.

Snaring

William Wordsworth

Snaring and Skating are extracts from Wordsworth's long autobiographical poem The Prelude which is subtitled the Growth of a poet's mind. In this poem he tells of events in his life which made him into the person he now is.

> Fair seed-time had my soul, and I grew up
> Fostered alike by beauty and by fear:
> Much favoured in my birth-place, and no less
> In that beloved Vale to which ere long
> We were transplanted; — there were we let loose
> For sports of wider range. Ere I had told
> Ten birth-days, when among the mountain-slopes
> Frost, and the breath of frosty wind, had snapped
> The last autumnal crocus, 'twas my joy
> With store of springes o'er my shoulder hung
> To range the open heights where woodcocks run
> Among the smooth green turf. Through half the night,
> Scudding away from snare to snare, I plied
> That anxious visitation; — moon and stars
> Were shining o'er my head. I was alone,
> And seemed to be a trouble to the peace
> That dwelt among them. Sometimes it befell
> In these night wanderings, that a strong desire
> O'erpowered my better reason, and the bird
> Which was the captive of another's toil
> Became my prey; and when the deed was done
> I heard among the solitary hills
> Low breathings coming after me, and sounds
> Of undistinguishable motion, steps
> Almost as silent as the turf they trod.

■ *Language and Concepts*

Blank Verse
Blank Verse is verse that is unrhymed. To be verse, however, it must have some regularity of rhythm or metre. The most common metre in English poetry is the iambic which consists of an unstressed syllable followed by a stressed syllable.

   /   /   /   /   /
To range the open heights where wood cocks run

1   'Fair-seed time had my soul, and I grew up
    Fostered alike by beauty and by fear.'

    From this extract show how the young Wordsworth was
    influenced 'by beauty and by fear'.

2   Wordsworth feels that he is somehow intruding on the peace
    of nature. Pick out the lines where this feeling is evident.

3   When he had stolen birds from somebody else's snares what
    does he experience from his surroundings?

4   Wordsworth said that poetry should be written in the 'real
    language of men'. How colloquial is the language of this
    extract?

5   What kind of boy was the young Wordsworth?

Skating

William Wordsworth

And in the frosty season, when the sun
Was set, and visible for many a mile
The cottage windows blazed through twilight gloom,
I heeded not their summons: happy time
It was indeed for all of us — for me
It was a time of rapture! Clear and loud
The village clock tolled six, — I wheeled about,
Proud and exulting like an untired horse
That cares not for his home. All shod with steel,
We hissed along the polished ice in games
Confederate, imitative of the chase
And woodland pleasures — the resounding horn,
The pack loud chiming, and the hunted hare.
So through the darkness and the cold we flew,
And not a voice was idle; with the din
Smitten, the precipices rang aloud;
The leafless trees and every icy crag
Tinkled like iron; while far distant hills
Into the tumult sent an alien sound
Of melancholy not unnoticed, while the stars
Eastward were sparkling clear, and in the west
The orange sky of evening died away.

Not seldom from the uproar I retired
Into a silent bay, or sportively
Glanced sideway, leaving the tumultuous throng,
To cut across the reflex of a star
That fled, and, flying still before me, gleamed
Upon the glassy plain; and oftentimes,
When we had given our bodies to the wind,
And all the shadowy banks on either side
Came sweeping through the darkness, spinning still
The rapid line of motion, then at once
Have I, reclining back upon my heels,
Stopped short; yet still the solitary cliffs
Wheeled by me — even as if the earth had rolled
With visible motion her diurnal round!
Behind me did they stretch in solemn train,
Feebler and feebler, and I stood and watched
Till all was tranquil as a dreamless sleep.

■ *Readings and Responses*

1   Show how it was 'a time of rapture' for the young Wordsworth.

2   In line ten there is a word which conveys the sound of skates. What is it? What is the name given to a word which makes the sound it is describing?

3   Wordsworth is willing to take part in boisterous activity but he is also something of an outsider. Show where both aspects of his personaltiy are evident in the poem.

4   At the end he experiences a feeling of great calm and tranquillity. What brings this feeling about?

5   Describe a boisterous game you have engaged in. In a paragraph put in as many 'active' words as possible.

WAR

∎

In human life it is said that there is the horror, the glory and the boredom. War surely represents the horror at its worst because war not only means outrageous human suffering but it also represents man's failure. It is said that the first casualty in war is truth. If that is so, then language is also a casualty because language is distorted in order to tell lies and to hide the truth. For example, in the Gulf War the term 'collateral damage' was used to hide the horror of civilian deaths. Poets write about war in order to understand it, in order to express its horror and as a warning.

The Leveller

The Patriot

Dulce et Decorum Est

Base Details

O What is that Sound?

Pigtail

∎

The Leveller

Robert Graves

Near Martinpuich that night of Hell
Two men were struck by the same shell,
Together tumbling in one heap
Senseless and limp like slaughtered sheep.

One was a pale eighteen-year-old,
Blue-eyed and thin and not too bold,
Pressed for the war not ten years too soon,
The shame and pity of his platoon.

The other came from far-off lands
With bristling chin and whiskered hands,
He had known death and hell before
In Mexico and Ecuador.

Yet in his death this cut-throat wild
Groaned 'Mother! Mother!' like a child,
While that poor innocent in man's clothes
died cursing God with brutal oaths.

Old Sergeant Smith, kindest of men,
Wrote out two copies, there and then
Of his accustomed funeral speech
To cheer the womenfolk of each: —

'He died a hero's death: and we
His Comrades of 'A' Company
Deeply regret his death: we shall
All deeply miss so dear a pal.'

■ *Readings and Responses*

1 Describe the contrasting characters of the two men as described in verses two and three.

2 Was their attitudes at the time of their deaths somewhat surprising?

3 It is said that in war the first casualty is truth. What is meant by this statement? Is the truth of this statement illustrated, to some degree, in this poem?

4 Was Sergeant Smith right to send the letter to the families?

5 What do you think is meant by the title?

The Patriot

Robert Browning

I

It was roses, roses, all the way,
  With myrtle mixed in my path like mad:
The house-roofs seemed to heave and sway,
  The church-spires flamed, such flags they had,
A year ago on this very day.

II

The air broke into a mist with bells,
  The old walls rocked with the crowd and cries.
Had I said, "Good folk, mere noise repels —
  But give me your sun from yonder skies!"
They had answered, "And afterward, what else?"

III

Alack, it was I who leaped at the sun
  To give it my loving friends to keep!
Naught man could do, have I left undone:
  And you see my harvest, what I reap
This very day, now a year is run.

IV

There's nobody on the house-tops now —
  Just a palsied few at the windows set:
For the best of the sight is, all allow,
  At the Shambles Gate — or, better yet,
By the very scaffold's foot, I trow.

V

I go in the rain, and, more than needs,
  A rope cuts both my wrists behind;
And I think, by the feel, my forehead bleeds,
  For they fling, whoever has a mind,
Stones at me for my year's misdeeds.

VI

Thus I entered, and thus I go!
  In triumphs, people have dropped down dead.
"Paid by the world, what dost thou owe
  Me?" God might question; now instead,
'Tis God shall repay; I am safer so.

1   In the first two verses the patriot is being acclaimed by the crowd. Which detail most vividly conveys the sense of triumphant celebration?

2   'Alack, it was I who leaped at the sun'

    What do you think is meant by these lines? What do they tell us about the kind of man the patriot was?

3   The fourth and fifth verses describe the complete reversal of the patriot's position. Which detail do you find most poignant (touching)?

4   Does this poem have anything to tell us about life in general?

5   What exactly is a patriot? Try to analyse the word and what it might have meant historically and what it might mean in the modern world.

Dulce et Decorum Est

Wilfred Owen

Bent double, like old beggars under sacks,
Knock-kneed, coughing like hags, we cursed through sludge,
Till on the haunting flares we turned our backs,
And towards our distant rest began to trudge.
Men marched asleep. Many had lost their boots,
But limped on, blood-shod. All went lame, all blind;
Drunk with fatigue; deaf even to the hoots
Of gas-shells dropping softly behind.

Gas! Gas! Quick, boys! — An ecstasy of fumbling,
Fitting the clumsy helmets just in time,
But someone still was yelling out and stumbling
And floundering like a man in fire or lime. —
Dim through the misty panes and thick green light,
As under a green sea, I saw him drowning.

In all my dreams before my helpless sight
He plunges at me, guttering, choking, drowning.

If in some smothering dreams, you too could pace
Behind the wagon that we flung him in,
And watch the white eyes writhing in his face,
His hanging face, like a devil's sick of sin;
If you could hear, at every jolt, the blood
Come gargling from the froth-corrupted lungs,
Bitter as the cud
Of vile, incurable sores on innocent tongues, —
My friend, you would not tell with such high zest
To children ardent for some desperate glory,
The old lie: *Dulce et decorum est
Pro patria mori.*

■ *Language and Concepts*

Emotion and order in poetry
A poet may want to express his/her deepest emotion on some
subject such as love, or grief, or horror. In the poem above,
Wilfred Owen, who himself fought in the First World War and
witnessed at first hand the horrors of the trenches, wants to
express his detestation of the obscenity of war. However, a
spontaneous gush of emotion in an uncontrolled manner would
not have the same power as the combination of the deepest
emotion ordered by rhyme, metre and structure.

■ *Readings and Responses*

1   Soldiers marching: what are they meant to look like? In what
    state are they meant to keep their equipment, their uniforms?
    What hellish contrast is presented in the first verse?

2   Look at the word 'blood-shod'. What does it suggest in your
    mind?

3   Pick out what you think is the most memorable and vivid
    word or image in the last section. Give your reasons.

4   This poem has powerful emotion but it is also carefully
    constructed. Look at the rhymes, the metre, and the climax.

5   What is this poem saying about patriotism, pacificism, a just
    war? Analyse what is meant by these words.

Base Details

Siegfried Sassoon

If I were fierce, and bald, and short of breath,
　　I'd live with scarlet Majors at the Base,
And speed the glum heroes up the line to death.
　　You'd see me with my puffy, petulant face,
Guzzling and gulping in the best hotel,
　　Reading the roll of Honour, "Poor young chap,"
I'd say — "I used to know his father well;
　　Yes, we've lost heavily in this last scrap."
And when the war is done and youth stone dead,
I'd toddle safely home and die — in bed.

■ *Language and Concepts*

Satire
Satire is the act of attacking the foolishness and vices of people by using sarcasm, mockery, humour or abuse. Satire can be gentle or bitter, elegant or brutal. The satirist is trying to show how the world could be better if only humankind lived up to its ideals. The satirist is very aware of the gap between what persons say and what they do; he/she is very aware of the gap between what humanity could be and what humanity is.

■ *Readings and Responses*

1　Write a short character sketch of the person in this poem. Include what he looks like and what his attitudes are.

2　What does the word 'scarlet' as used in line two suggest to you?

3　What is suggested by the word 'toddle' in the last line?

4　Read the poem aloud. Try to match the feeling in the poem with your tone of voice. How would you describe the tone of the satire?

5　What relationship between ordinary soldiers and their generals is suggested in this poem? Do you think the poet is fair to both groups?

O What is that Sound?
(The Quarry)
W. H. Auden

O what is that sound which so thrills the ear
Down in the valley drumming, drumming?
Only the scarlet soldiers, dear,
The soldiers coming.

O what is that light I see flashing so clear
Over the distance brightly, brightly?
Only the sun on their weapons, dear,
As they step lightly.

O what are they doing with all that gear,
What are they doing this morning, this morning?
Only the usual manoeuvres, dear,
Or perhaps a warning.

O why have they left the road down there,
Why are they suddenly wheeling, wheeling?
Perhaps a change in the orders, dear,
Why are you kneeling?

O haven't they stopped for the doctor's care,
Haven't they reined their horses, their horses?
Why, there are none of them wounded, dear,
None of these forces.

O is it the parson they want, with white hair,
Is the parson, is it, is it?
No, they are passing his gateway, dear,
Without a visit.

O it must be the farmer who lives so near;
It must be the farmer so cunning, so cunning.
They have passed the farm already, dear,
And now they are running.

O where are you going? Stay with me here!
Were the vows you swore me deceiving, deceiving?
No, I promised to love you, dear,
But I must be leaving.

O it's broken the lock and splintered the door,
O it's the gate where they're turning, turning;
Their boots are heavy on the floor
And their eyes are burning.

Tension

A sense of tension is built up when we don't know what is going to happen. In a football or hockey match there is no tension if one team is winning so easily that we know what is going to happen. There is tension in the match if the result is doubtful. Tension thus exists when the situation is unclear but something important is going to happen. Tension could occur when a person has an important decision to make such as whether to marry one person rather than another. Tension occurs when we don't know the outcome of a struggle or a conflict or when a major change is going to take place. Once we know what is going to happen, once the decision is made, once the result of the struggle or conflict is known, once the change has taken place, the tension is dissolved. Almost all novels, stories and dramas involve this creation of tension and its ultimate resolution.

■ *Readings and Responses*

1   Read the poem aloud with a different pupil reading each of the two speakers in the poem. How many speakers are there in the last verse? Why?

2   Does the rhythm, the beat of the lines, suggest anything to you?

3   How is the tension created? Look at all the questions asked and read carefully the note on tension above.

4   Look at the second last verse. What kind of betrayal takes place here?

5   Look at the last verse. What kind of society does the poem suggest? Why is the word 'it's' used?

Pigtail

Tadeusz Rózewicz
Trans: Adam Czerniawski

When all the women in the transport
had their heads shaved
four workmen with brooms made of birch twigs
swept up
and gathered up the hair

Behind clean glass
the stiff hair lies
of those suffocated in gas chambers
there are pins and side combs
in this hair

The hair is not shot through with light
is not parted by the breeze
is not touched by any hand
or rain or lips
In huge chests
clouds of dry hair
of those suffocated
and a faded plait
a pigtail with a ribbon
pulled at school
by naughty boys.

The Museum, Auschwitz, 1948

■ *Readings and Responses*

1   Why do you think the hair of the women gassed in Auschwitz
is kept in the museum there?

2   Look at the third verse. What do you think the poet thinks of
when he looks at the hair in the glass cases of the museum?

3   Why is the pigtail with the ribbon particularly poignant and
moving?

4   Compare this poem with any other poem in this section.
Which of them manages to convey its message more
powerfully?

5   The pigtail comes to represent all the human life and human
potentiality which was destroyed by the Holocaust. If you
were to put five objects in a time capsule to represent life as it
is lived today, what five objects would you choose? Try to
range over all aspects of modern life.